An
Theologians on Covenant
and Baptism
by Jelle Faber

&

Extra-Scriptural Binding
— A New Danger
by Klaas Schilder

INHERITANCE PUBLICATIONS
NEERLANDIA, ALBERTA, CANADA
PELLA, IOWA, U.S.A.

American Secession Theologians on Covenant and Baptism
by Jelle Faber

&

Extra-Scriptural Binding — A New Danger
by Klaas Schilder

INHERITANCE PUBLICATIONS
NEERLANDIA, ALBERTA, CANADA
PELLA, IOWA, U.S.A.

Canadian Cataloguing in Publication Data
Faber, Jelle, 1924-
  American secession theologians on covenant and baptism / Jelle
Faber. Extra-scriptural binding—a new danger / Klaas Schilder
  Includes index.
  ISBN 0-921100-46-9
    1. Covenants—religious aspects—Reformed Church. 2. Covenant
  theology. 3. Baptism—Reformed Church. 4. Reformed Church—
  doctrines. I. Schilder, Klaas, 1890-1952. Extra-scriptural binding—
  a new danger. I. Title: American secession theologians on
  covenant and baptism.
BX9422.5.f32 1996   231.7'6   C96-910143-0

Library of Congress Cataloging-in-Publication Data
Faber, J. (Jelle), 1924-
  American Secession theologians on covenant and baptism / by
Jelle Faber. Extra-scriptural Binding : a new danger / by Klaas
Schilder.
    p. cm.
  Extra-scriptural binding is "a translation of a series of articles that
  appeared in De Reformatie in the Netherlands"— p.
  ISBN 0-921100-46-9
    1. Covenants—Religious aspects—Reformed Church—History of
  doctrines. 2. Election (Theology)—History of doctrines.
  3. Baptism—Reformed Church. 4. Nederlandse Hervormde Kerk—
  history—Secession, 1834. 5. Doleantie, 1886. 6. Reformed
  Church—United States—Doctrines—History—19th century.
  7. Reformed Church—United States—Doctrines—History—
  20th century. 8. Reformed Church—Netherlands—Doctrines—
  History—19th century. 9. Reformed Church—Netherlands—
  Doctrines—History—20th century.
I. Schilder, K. (Klaas), 1890-1952. Selections. English. 1996.
  II. Title.
BT155.f33   1996
231.7'6—dc20   96-7626
                                                    CIP

Cover Picture by Roelof A. Janssen

Published simultaneously in U.S.A. by Inheritance Publications
Box 366, Pella, Iowa 50219 Tel. & Fax (515) 628 3804

Printed in Canada by Premier Printing Ltd. Winnipeg, MB

Contents

Publisher's Preface 7

Jelle Faber
*American Secession Theologians
on Covenant and Baptism* 15

Klaas Schilder
Extra-Scriptural Binding — A New Danger

1. Occasion and Reason 57
2. Clear Doctrine? 72
3. Rightly Dividing 74
4. The Voice of the Fathers of Dort 76
5. Be Careful with Dictionaries 77
6. Bad *Condition* Theories 78
7. Good *Condition* Theory 80
8. Summary 81
9. A New Point 82
10. *Cause* or Ground? 82
11. "Cause," a Term Easily Misunderstood 85
12. *Beginning* of the Work of Grace in Us 87
13. Theorems 88
14. Infallible Concern 88
15. Dogmatic Statement or Address? 89
16. Are For 90
17. Common Grace 91
18. Heynsianism 93
19. An Old Statement 94
20. Maintained Statement 100
21. What is Behind it? 101
22. Concern 105
23. Gracious Offer 106
24. Supralapsarianism? 107
25. Apparently 109
26. Disposition 110
27. Beza on Decree and Execution of the Decree 112
28. Promise or Gift-Without-Strings Attached:
    a Matter of Stipulation 114

29. Beza About *Concern* 115
30. Beza About *Grace* and *Offer* 115
31. Beza's Sketch 117
32. God, Offering Himself 118
33. Condition and Threat 118
34. Calling and Decree 119
35. Summary Regarding Beza 121
36. Addition Concerning Beza 122
37. Preface to the *Staten Bijbel* 125
38. Must an Opinion Literally be Found in the Confession? 126
39. The Better Question 128
40. An Example 128
41. Conditions and *Dort* 130
42. Conditions and Canons 131
43. Details from the Canons 133
44. Character of the Promise 134
45. Promising is *Saying* 136
46. *Saying* with Authority 136
47. *Earnest* 138
48. What Kind of Oath? 139
49. An Oath of Assertion of a Common Truth? 140
50. *About* the Elect, or *To* the Called? 140
51. Quality and Address of the Oath: Two Central Questions 141
52. To *Will* 143
53. To You 145
54. *Are,* or also *Become*? 146
55. Conclusion on this Point 146
56. God's Reliability at Stake 147
57. The Dangerous Art of Syllogism 148
58. Uncertain Baptism 149
59. No More Threat? 150
60. To *Conclude* About God, or About Oneself? 151
61. Isaiah About God's Truthfulness 151
62. Provisional Closing Remarks 152
63. Correspondence 163

Scripture Index 168
General Index 169

Publisher's Preface

In a time of much confusion about Church and Covenant it is our pleasure to provide a book that wants to shed a clear Biblical light on these issues. Not only does Dr. Jelle Faber show that the Canadian and American Reformed Churches stand in the tradition of the Christian Reformed Church, the translation of Dr. Klaas Schilder's articles on extra-Scriptural binding[1] show that the Church today should oppose any such binding.

It is evident that there is a great need for an English publication of these latter articles. Voices have been heard from the Protestant Reformed Churches that Klaas Schilder did not want to respond [in *De Reformatie*] to Herman Hoeksema's articles.[2]

Dr. Schilder wrote these articles with the purpose of preventing the Dutch immigrants of the (liberated)

---

[1] The Dutch title of Schilder's brochure [which was a slightly revised edition of his articles in *De Reformatie*] was: *Bovenschriftuurlijke binding — een nieuw gevaar* (Binding above Scripture [or: Supra Scriptural binding] — A New Danger. Throughout these two essays we have used the term extra-Scriptural binding.

[2] Rev. B. Woudenberg has written several articles in *The Standard Bearer* in which he repeatedly stated that Schilder was not inclined to give definite answers on the differences between Hoeksema and himself. In September of 1993 I talked with Rev. Woudenberg and asked him if he had ever seen the responses of Schilder in *De Reformatie*. He told me that his reading abilities in Dutch were not very good. I told him that Schilder had written extensively about the matter. Nevertheless, Rev. Woudenberg repeated the same things in his response to Rev. Jelle Tuininga, published in *Christian Renewal*, Oct. 13, 1995, and in *The Standard Bearer*, Nov. 15, 1995. The truth of the matter is that Schilder quoted (in translation) Hoeksema extensively in *De Reformatie*, while Hoeksema did not do the same in *The Standard Bearer*.

Reformed Churches from being forced to establish a separate church federation. Throughout his articles he warns against extra-Scriptural binding, a warning that also the Canadian Reformed Churches at the end of the 20th century should take to heart. Both Dr. Faber and Dr. Schilder clearly state in this book that there is no "liberated" theology, not on the Covenant and not on the Church. We believe what the Bible teaches and confess it in the Three Forms of Unity. No church may hinder God's children from becoming members when those children submit to God's Word. In seeking unity on Biblical principles with other churches let us also be careful not to bind where Scripture does not bind, only then will we be faithful instruments in bringing together what belongs together. It is our sincere conviction that even today the Canadian/American Reformed Churches should be united with the Protestant Reformed Churches (if, at least, the *Declaration of Principles* will be removed) as well as with the Free Reformed Churches, the Orthodox Christian Reformed Churches, the Independent Reformed Churches, and other churches that submit to God's Word.

It is our prayer that God will use the publication of this booklet for the glory of His Name and the edifying of His people.

We would like to thank Mr. T. Van Laar for translating the booklet of Schilder. Even though his work has been thoroughly edited the initial work was much appreciated. Many changes were made in order to state more clearly what the author intended. Anyone familiar with the original Dutch writings of Schilder will know how difficult it is to translate his masterful use of the language. His play on words often makes it — even in Dutch — hard to understand, especially when one is not familiar with his style and other writings. We therefore want to express appreciation to Dr. Faber, Mr. & Mrs. A. Viersen, and my wife Theresa for the many hours they have spent in editing and re-editing the second part of this booklet. Although we do not claim it to be a perfect translation, we do believe it to be a very responsible translation.

Some further words of thanks are due to Professor David Engelsma of the Protestant Reformed Seminary, to my nephew, Karlo Janssen, who is a student at the Theological College of the Canadian Reformed Churches, and to Dr. Harry Boonstra, Theological Librarian at Calvin Theological Seminary, for faxing us reference material needed for this book.

Neerlandia, Alberta   Roelof A. Janssen

American
Secession
Theologians
On Covenant
and Baptism

Jelle Faber

This essay was written for the
140th anniversary of the
Theological University in Kampen
and a ministers' workshop at the
Theological College in Hamilton.

It is dedicated to the memory of
Prof. Lubbertus Selles
(1915-1993).
Born in Kampen, he emigrated to
Ontario in 1952.

AMERICAN SECESSION THEOLOGIANS ON COVENANT AND BAPTISM

Three historic occasions

The decisive moment for the publication of this essay was determined by three historic occasions.

First, on December 6, 1994, the Theological University in Kampen, the Netherlands, celebrated its 140th anniversary. My *alma mater* is a monument of the Secession, the reformational movement of the year 1834. The theological seminary in Kampen, established in 1854, is often called "the School of the Secession." The topic of this essay accordingly deals with theologians of the Secession.

Second, 1994 was also the year in which the *Vrijmaking* was commemorated. This *Vrijmaking*, or Liberation, of 1944 — half a century ago — was a reformational movement in the Reformed Churches of the Netherlands in the twentieth century. In respect of doctrine this Liberation had to do with synodical pronouncements, especially with those that dealt with the covenant of grace.[1] The topic of this publication, therefore, is connected with the doctrines of God's covenant and baptism.

Last but not least, 1969 was the year that the Theological College of the Canadian Reformed Churches was established in Hamilton, Ontario, and as theologians of Dutch descent we celebrated our twenty-fifth anniversary on the American continent. My topic, therefore, deals with immigrant theologians: American Reformed theologians of Dutch descent.

Combining the three historic occasions we come to the theme:

---

[1] See the first of three addresses given in October 1994 that were dedicated to the commemoration of the Liberation of 1944, published in C. Van Dam, ed., *The Liberation: Causes and Consequences* (Winnipeg: Premier Printing, 1995).

15

AMERICAN SECESSION THEOLOGIANS
ON COVENANT AND BAPTISM

The name "Secession theologians" is meant in the strict sense of "theologians who had been members of the church of the Secession in the Netherlands." Therefore, they must have lived in the period of 1834 till 1892 in what some of the Reformed people in North America still call "the old country."

The year 1892 saw one of the "miracles" of the nineteenth century. This "miracle" was the union of Reformed confessors in the church of the Secession and in the churches of the *Doleantie*, the second reformational movement (1886) in the Netherlands.

Our topic deals with "*American* Secession theologians" not only because all of them immigrated to America but also because I restrict myself to some of their American publications.

Moreover, the title does not speak about *the* American Secession theologians but about some of them. We limit ourselves to seven American Secession theologians.

According to traditional homiletic custom we divide the topic into three parts.

First we deal with the *individuals*, that is, the persons and the publications of these American Secession theologians; secondly we deal with their *insights* on covenant and baptism; and thirdly we deal with their *influence* in or impact on the history of Reformed theology, especially in the work of Dr. Klaas Schilder.

We also use the formula of an historic, a doctrinal, and a practical part, or rather, we deal with,
American Secession theologians on covenant and baptism

    I. their individualities
    II. their insights
    III. their influence

I. INDIVIDUALITIES

Who were these American Secession theologians and what did they publish?

We enumerate them not in the order of their year of birth but of their arrival in what was then still called "the new world." Let us call it the year of their second civil birth.

We deal then with Geert Egberts Boer (1873), Lammert Jan Hulst (1874), Gerrit Klaas Hemkes (1877), Geerhardus Vos (1881), William Wijnand Heyns (1882), Hendericus Beuker (1893), and finally Foppe Martin ten Hoor (1896).[2]

I chose this "group of seven" not only in connection with their publications on covenant and baptism but also to emphasize the historical continuity between theological institutions: Kampen, Grand Rapids, and Hamilton. Five of these seven American Secession theologians studied in Kampen, namely, Boer, Hemkes, Heyns, Beuker, and Ten Hoor. The five mentioned above, and Vos, taught in Grand Rapids, Michigan, and all seven, including *Domine* L. J. Hulst, are still honoured in Hamilton. Hulst was a remarkable theologian in his own right and he co-authored with Prof. G. K. Hemkes a few publications that we cannot bypass when we deal with our topic.

Since their *curricula vitae* are not well known anymore, not even to the present generation of Reformed theologians, I cannot but tell something about the life and publications of these modest, humble, and nevertheless interesting and, above all, God fearing brothers.[3]

---

[2] For biographical and bibliographical data see the first and the second edition of *Christelijke Encyclopedie* (Kampen: Kok, 1925, 1956), s.v., and Peter de Klerk, *A Bibliography of the Writings of the Professors of Calvin Theological Seminary* (Grand Rapids: Calvin Theological Seminary, 1980). Peter de Klerk, librarian emeritus, kindly photocopied rare lecture notes. Those of Vos, Beuker, and Heyns can now also be consulted in the library of the Theological College of the Canadian Reformed Churches in Hamilton.

[3] One should also consult H. Zwaanstra, *Reformed Thought and Experience in a New World*. A study of the Christian Reformed Church and its American environment 1890-1918 (Kampen: Kok, 1973), with its Selected Bibliography and its Index of Names.

1. The first is **Geert Egberts Boer** (1832-1904).

Born in 1832, he finished his studies in Kampen in 1865 on the same day as his later colleague Hemkes. Geert Boer crossed the Ocean in 1873 and when three years later, in 1876, the Theological School in Grand Rapids was established, he was its first and only professor. In 1884 — therefore, eight years later — Hemkes became the second professor. For years the two men delivered more than fifty lectures per week, while at the same time they edited the weekly *de Wachter*.

Boer's first publication in *de Wachter* was a letter to Helenius de Cock in Kampen. In 1875 he wrote articles on baptism, on Genesis 17 in connection with Romans 9, and on Lord's Day 26 of the Heidelberg Catechism. Of his many publications in *de Wachter* I mention as yet the series of (Dutch) letters "To my friend L. in the Netherlands" (1893). One will not be mistaken to see in this friend L. Professor Lukas Lindeboom in Kampen. Around the turn of this century G. E. Boer wrote about infant baptism and about the expression "sanctified in Christ." He regarded being sanctified in Christ as the forensic ground of baptism (*de rechtsgrond van de doop*).

Having taught in Grand Rapids for twenty-six years, Geert Egberts Boer died in 1904.[4]

2. The second person in our series of American Secession theologians is the colourful figure of **Lammert J. Hulst** (1825-1922) who immigrated in 1874, a year after Boer.

---

[4] At the occasion of my inaugural address in 1969 a Free Reformed minister, the Rev. J. Overduin, presented to me the book *Een man des volks. Het leven van Prof. Geert Egberts Boer naar aanteekeningen uit zijn dagboek samengesteld door Prof. G. K. Hemkes* (A man of the people. The life of Prof. Geert Egberts Boer as compiled from his diary by Prof. G. K. Hemkes — Editor's note: translations of titles do not indicate that such a book has been published in English, but are only meant to help the reader understand the title itself) (Grand Rapids: J. B. Hulst, 1904). Undoubtedly the Rev. Overduin saw a parallel between 1876, the modest beginning of the Theological School in Grand Rapids and 1969, the sober start of the Theological College in Hamilton. He probably also noticed a similarity between *de domine van de Ware Hollandsche Gereformeerde Kerk* (the minister of the True Dutch Reformed Church) — as the name still read — and the new minister of a Canadian Reformed Church almost a century later. Also about Boer see the first chapter "Forgotten Benefactors" in J. J. Timmerman, *Promises to Keep. A Centennial History of Calvin College* (Grand Rapids, 1975).

L. J. Hulst was born in 1825 and died in 1922, ninety-seven years old. His captivating autobiography is entitled *A preacher for sixty-three years*. The former shepherd of Oud Leussen, in the neighbourhood of Dalfsen, was trained by the Rev. W. A. Kok in Hoogeveen. In 1849 he graduated from this "manse" training — five years before the Theological School in Kampen was even established. Hulst tells us interesting stories about his youth and his training. It shows that in Hoogeveen dogmatics and especially the *Marrow* of Francken took pride of place.[5] Hulst started his study of the biblical languages only after he had entered the manse, first in Birdaard with a son-in-law of Rev. T. F. de Haan and when he had accepted a call to Ferwerd in 1855, he walked every week to the Rev. J. R. Kreulen in Hallum for what he calls his "weekly conversation." Hulst writes about his Ferwerd period: "I underwent not only a change in the course of my studies but of even more significance was my change with respect to my view of the Covenant" (*mijne wijziging ten aanzien van mijne* VERBONDSopvatting). Lammert J. Hulst changed over from a *supra*lapsarian into an *infra*lapsarian and this had an impact on his entire long later life.[6]

In this treatise about covenant and baptism I need to tell how in Ferwerd Hulst refused to baptize a lad who was fourteen years old.

There was a family who wanted to join the congregation. There were eight children of whom only one was baptized. Hulst inquired and discovered that the eldest of the unbaptized children was fourteen years old. "I made the remark that he could not be baptized as a child anymore as the

---

[5] Hulst means A. Francken, *Kern der Christelyke Leere* (1719). The entry in *C.E.*, 2. ed., s.v., calls him akin to Voetius and Johannes a Marck and characterizes his writings as tainted by mysticism.

[6] *Drie en zestig jaren prediker. Gedenkschriften van Ds. Lammert J. Hulst* (Kampen: Kok, 1913), p. 57. Cf. H. M. Yoo, *Raad en daad. Infra- en supralapsarisme in de nederlandse Gereformeerde theologie van de 19e en 20e eeuw* (Kampen, 1990), s.v. Hulst. See for supra- and infralapsarianism in general H. Bavinck, *The Doctrine of God*, tr. W. Hendriksen (Edinburgh: Banner of Truth, 1977), pp. 382-394; L. Berkhof, *Systematic theology* (Grand Rapids: Eerdmans, 1953), pp. 118-125. In general, supralapsarianism places the decree of predestination above (supra) the decree to permit the fall (lapsus); while infralapsarianism places the decree of predestination proper below (infra) the decree to permit the fall.

other six children. The family was flabbergasted, but finally everything turned out well. Two years later the lad requested baptism on his own account, and when the elders had examined him, nobody dared to refuse this request, although the lad was now only sixteen years old. After his baptism he continued learning, first with Rev. Hulst, then in Kampen. The lad's name was Douwe Klaas Wielenga; as professor he became an asset for the Theological School in Kampen. All of his six sons became ministers and missionaries in the Reformed Churches. One of them was the father of my Kampen instructor in missiology, the unique "D.K.W." This Douwe Klaas Wielenga Jr. became the father and grandfather of two ministers in the Canadian and American Reformed Churches. One studied in Kampen, the other in Hamilton. Here we see Gods's covenant and baptism in the reality of the life of one of our American Secession theologians.[7]

Hulst made the cross-over to "the new world" in 1874 and became a minister, first, in the Reformed Church in America and, after his suspension in 1882, in the Christian Reformed Church.

This suspension was caused by his strong opposition against the Free Masonry. This struggle not only brought many members and congregations into the Christian Reformed Church but also occasioned a change in the ecclesiastical position of the Seceded Synod of Zwolle, 1882, with respect to the gathering of the true church in America.[8]

---

[7] *Drie en zestig jaren prediker. Gedenkschriften van Ds. Lammert J. Hulst* (Kampen, 1913), pp. 69-72.

[8] Yet as of 1873 Prof. A. Brummelkamp, brother-in-law of Rev. Albertus Van Raalte in Holland, Michigan, declared in a faculty meeting in Kampen that he rather went to the Reformed Church in America, while Prof. S. van Velzen chose for the True Holland Reformed Church. Cf. *Een man des volks. Het leven van Prof. Geert Egberts Boer.* Naar aanteekeningen uit zijn dagboek samengesteld door Prof. G. K. Hemkes (Grand Rapids: J. B. Hulst, 1904), p. 78. See about the struggle on membership of the Free Masonry also G. K. Hemkes, *Het rechtsbestaan der Holl. Chr. Geref. Kerk in Amerika* (Grand Rapids: Langereis and Hemkes, s.a. [1893?]), and E. J. Bruins, "The Masonic controversy in Holland, Michigan, 1879-1882" in P. de Klerk and R. R. de Ridder, eds., *Perspectives on the Christian Reformed Church. Studies in its history, theology, and ecumenicity* presented in honor of John Henry Kromminga (Grand Rapids: Baker, 1983), pp. 53-72.

Hulst as American Secession theologian is especially known for his publication *Supra en infra* in the year 1891. The sub-title reads: A word in defense and explanation of the Confessional Reformed doctrine and practice, concerning predestination and the covenant of grace.

Later, in 1913, he wrote with G. K. Hemkes the booklet *Oud- en nieuw calvinisme*. The titles of Hulst's publications make clear that he was a fervent opponent of supralapsarianism and therefore of Abraham Kuyper's view of the covenant.[9]

In 1917 Dr. J. van Lonkhuyzen defended this Kuyperian covenant view and was refuted by the Rev. Lammert J. Hulst in the brochure *Kentering in de verbondsleer* (Turning of the tide in the doctrine of the covenant).[10]

3. We can be more brief about number three: **Gerrit Klaas Hemkes** (1838-1920).

Born in 1838 and alumnus of Kampen in 1862, he departed for the United States in 1877. Hemkes accepted an appointment at the Theological School in Grand Rapids where he functioned mainly as church historian from 1884 - 1908. In 1886 he wrote a brochure about infant baptism, entitled *De kinderdoop uit God*. In 1913 he published a twofold pamphlet under the title *Onder of boven* (under or above) [and] *Kinderdoop IS Bijbelsch* (Infant Baptism *is* Biblical). The first part is directed against Supralapsarians, the second against Baptists and we do not have to belabour the fact that a theologian such as Hemkes saw a close connection between those two movements: Supralapsarianism and Anabaptism. We dealt already with his co-authorship with

---

[9] L. J. Hulst, *Supra en infra. Een woord van verdediging en toelichting der Confessioneel Gereformeerde leer en practijk, omtrent de praedestinatie en het genadeverbond* (Grand Rapids: Doornik & Zoon, 1891). L. J. Hulst and G. K. Hemkes, *Oud- en nieuw calvinisme. Tweeledige inlichting voor ons Hollandsche volk over Het oude en nieuwe calvinisme en De kerk* (Old and new Calvinism. A twofold information about the old and new Calvinism and the Church for our Dutch people) (Grand Rapids: Eerdmans-Sevensma, 1913).

[10] Dr. J. van Lonkhuyzen, *Heilig zaad. Verhandelingen over den Heiligen Doop* (Sanctified seed. A discourse on Holy Baptism) (Grand Rapids: n.d.); L. J. Hulst, *Kentering in de verbondsleer* (Holland, Michigan, 1917).

Hulst, although the reader gets the impression that *Oud en nieuw calvinisme* is mainly written by Lammert Hulst.[11]

4. Far more important than Hemkes is the following American Secession theologian, **Geerhardus Vos** (1862-1949).

Vos, born in 1862, matriculated from the *gymnasium* (grammar-school) in Amsterdam. In 1881, when he was nineteen years old, he emigrated with his parents to the land of "unlimited possibilities." He studied in Grand Rapids and then in Princeton, Berlin, and Strasbourg, where he obtained a Ph. D.

From 1888 till 1893 he was Professor of Dogmatics and Exegesis in Grand Rapids. Then he was appointed in Princeton for the second time (the first time he declined the appointment) and disappeared into the PCUS, the Presbyterian Church in the United States. Abraham Kuyper compared the transition of Herman Bavinck from Kampen to Amsterdam with the departure of Vos from Grand Rapids. He wrote to Bavinck that Vos probably went too far by going to the Presbyterians but he did certainly the right thing by leaving the small school (*het schooltje*) in Grand Rapids. "It would have meant academic murder."

In Princeton Vos became Professor of Biblical Theology from 1893 till 1932. Alas, he did not join the reformational movement that led to the establishing of the Orthodox Presbyterian Church in 1936. Dr. Cornelis Van Til told me that it was nevertheless he who was asked to lead the funeral service, when Geerhardus Vos died in 1949.[12]

His first period — the period in Grand Rapids — is especially important for our topic.

---

[11] G. K. Hemkes, *De kinderdoop uit God* (Grand Rapids, 1886); id., *Onder of boven [en] Kinderdoop is Bijbelsch. Een woord aan Ds.* (A word to Rev.) *W. R. Smidt* (Grand Rapids: Verhaar, 1913). See P. de Klerk, *op. cit.*, 12.12 and 12.27 for relevant articles by Hemkes in *de Wachter* and *de Gereformeerde Amerikaan.*

[12] See about life and significance of G. Vos especially the Introduction in R. B. Gaffin Jr., ed., *Redemptive History and Biblical Interpretation. The Shorter Writings of Geerhardus Vos* (Phillipsburg: Presbyterian & Reformed Publishing Co., 1980), pp. IX-XXIII. A. Kuyper's remark concerning G. Vos is found *ib.* p. XI, and in R. H. Bremmer, *Herman Bavinck en zijn tijdgenoten* (Herman Bavinck and his contemporaries) (Kampen: Kok, 1966), pp. 81, 291.

In 1891 Vos delivered a remarkable principal's address about *The doctrine of the covenant in Reformed theology.*[13] Far less known are Vos' important lecture notes, entitled *Gereformeerde dogmatiek* and *Systematische theologie.*

The first edition of Geerhardus Vos' Reformed dogmatics was a hectographed manuscript in five volumes (1888). A later 1910 edition is type-written. This *Gereformeerde dogmatiek* of Vos was never available for public sale. There is a copy in three U.S. seminaries (Calvin, Westminster, and Reformed Theological Seminary) and a newly made photocopy in the Theological College of the Canadian Reformed Churches in Hamilton.

The much shorter lecture notes entitled *Systematische theologie* is a compendium hectographed by Calvin Theological Seminary in 1895 and reproduced in 1896, 1905, 1909, and 1916. "Hamilton" has the editions of 1905 and 1916.[14]

5. We come to number five: **William Wijnand Heyns** (1856-1933).

Heyns was born in 1856, began his theological study in Kampen in the years 1877 till 1881 and then crossed the Ocean and finished his studies in Grand Rapids. He was Professor of Diaconiology at the seminary from 1902 till 1926, while at the same time, since 1904, Professor of Reformed Doctrine at Calvin College.

---

[13] G. Vos, *De verbondsleer in de Gereformeerde theologie*, was published by "Democrat" Drukpers at Grand Rapids in 1891 and reprinted by Mazijk's Uitgeversbureau in Rotterdam, 1939. Gaffin gave an English translation in *Redemptive History and Biblical Interpretation. The Shorter Writings of Geerhardus Vos* (Phillipsburg, 1980), pp. 234-267.

[14] J. J. Timmerman, *op. cit.*, p. 15 writes: "Dr. Vos was a brilliant scholar and teacher whose impact on the minds of his students proved to be permanent. His mimeographed notes were abiding treasures to his students." In 1952 an English version of the section of Vos' *Dogmatiek* about God's decrees was published in *Reformed Review*. See P. de Klerk *op. cit.* 40.1. We mention for Vos' later period the article "Covenant" in J. Hastings, ed., *A Dictionary of Christ and the Gospels* (New York, 1906), 1:373-380. See further the essays " 'Covenant' or 'Testament'?" (1914) and "Hebrews, the Epistle of the Diatheke" (1915) in *Redemptive History and Biblical Interpretation. The shorter writings of Geerhardus Vos*, pp. 400-411, 161-233.

In 1889, 1899, and following years he published articles that he later used for a now rare series of lecture notes entitled *Verhandelingen over het genadeverbond* (Essays on the covenant of grace). In 1903 Heyns wrote also on the Form for Baptism in his *Liturgiek* (Liturgics). Also his *Handboek voor de catechetiek* (Catechetics, 1907) is important for our topic.

Heyns became especially well known through his book *Gereformeerde geloofsleer*. It appeared in 1916 in the Netherlands with a laudatory preface by Prof. H. Bouwman of Kampen. It was translated not only into English as *Manual of Reformed doctrine* (1926) but also into Hungarian.

In the first sentence Heyns characterizes his *Manual* as "a compendium of the truths concerning salvation which are revealed to us in the Holy Scriptures, and which we have to know and to believe as participants of the covenant of grace, since this knowledge is indispensable in order to walk in the way of the covenant and to inherit its benefits."[15] It is clear that Heyns deserves our attention on points of doctrine.

But we first have to deal with two late-comers among the American Secession theologians: Hendericus Beuker and Foppe Martin ten Hoor.

While the other individuals arrived during the seventies or the beginning of the eighties, it is not without cause that these last two men departed from the Netherlands *after* the Union of the Reformed Churches in 1892, and travelled to America as the land of the free. They probably did not want to live under the dominance of the theology of Abraham Kuyper.

6. Number six is then **Hendericus Beuker** (1834-1900).

Born in the year of the Secession, 1834, Beuker obtained his diploma in Kampen in 1865. After having been minister, founder, and editor of the journal *De Vrije Kerk* (The Free Church) in the Netherlands, he was almost sixty years of age, when he immigrated to the United States. Beuker succeeded Geerhardus Vos and served as Professor of Dogmatics in Grand Rapids.

---

[15] See for Heyns' publications esp. P. de Klerk, *op. cit.*, 14.1-14.5, 14.10-14.11. Interesting for our topic is also a series of articles *Behoort het bezit van wedergeboorte tot het in-zijn in het genade-verbond?"* (Does the possession of regeneration belong to the in-being in the covenant of grace?) in *de Wachter* of 1918, P. de Klerk, *op. cit.* 14.12.

In 1897/98 he wrote in the weekly *De Gereformeerde Amerikaan* (The Reformed American) a series of articles about God's covenantal government (*God's verbonds-bestuur*), but more important are his now rare college notes from 1898, entitled *Gereformeerde dogmatiek* (Reformed Dogmatics).[16]

7. Our last American Secession theologian is **Foppe Martin ten Hoor** (1855-1934).

Ten Hoor obtained the Kampen diploma in 1880. It was on the same day as Herman Bavinck, who in 1895 extensively corresponded with his contemporary and class-mate, discussing the principles of sacred theology and especially Abraham Kuyper's masterwork. Kuyper's *Principles of Sacred Theology* were prescribed to first year students during the first twenty-five years of the Theological College in Hamilton and thus Ten Hoor's objections are still being discussed.

When Ten Hoor arrived in America in 1896 he became founder of the publication *De Gereformeerde Amerikaan* and remained its editor for almost twenty years.

Ten Hoor succeeded Beuker as Professor of Dogmatics and he functioned as such at Calvin Theological Seminary from 1900 till 1924.

He is important for our topic especially through his *Compendium der Gereformeerde dogmatiek* (Summary of Reformed Dogmatics). At the end of his career, in 1922, Ten Hoor himself prepared this book of almost 300 pages. In the second part of this essay it will have our attention.[17]

---

[16] See Gerrit Jan Beuker, *Absgeschiedenes Streben nach Einheit: Leben und Wirken Henricus Beukers 1834-1900* (Kampen: Mondiss, 1996). K. Schilder wrote a sympathetic introduction to Beuker and his work in *De Reformatie*, 19:339. It does not become clear whether Schilder consulted Beuker's *Gereformeerde dogmatiek*. Schilder quotes Beuker from *De Gereformeerde Amerikaan*.

[17] F. M. ten Hoor, *Compendium der Gereformeerde dogmatiek. Een leiddraad voor studenten in de Theologie* (a guide for students of theology) (Holland, Mich.: A. ten Hoor, 1922). For the correspondence between Bavinck and Ten Hoor see: R. H. Bremmer, *Herman Bavinck als dogmaticus* (Kampen: Kok, 1961), pp. 46-54, 393-424; Id., *Herman Bavinck en zijn tijdgenoten* (Kampen: Kok, 1966), pp. 34f. Ten Hoor wrote some booklets about the difference between *Afscheiding* (Secession) (1834) and *Doleantie* (1886). For good reason the master's thesis of Cornelis Pronk is entitled *F. M. ten Hoor: Defender of Secession Principles Against Abraham Kuyper's Doleantie Views*

II. INSIGHTS

At the beginning of this doctrinal part we should keep a few things in mind. First, the word *covenant* in our theme does not refer to the so-called "covenant of redemption" or "counsel of peace" nor to the so-called "covenant of works" but to the covenant of grace. This is also indicated by the combination covenant and baptism.

Further, there is no Secession theology concerning covenant and baptism. There is no American Secession theology either.

For that matter there is no theology of the Liberation of 1944 in the Reformed Churches of the Netherlands and there is also no Canadian Reformed theology concerning covenant and baptism or concerning the church.

At the centenary of the Secession Doctor Klaas Schilder argued that there arose no sect in 1834, not in the church but also not in theology. The dogmatic or symbol-historical significance of the Secession was the return to the official documents of the church, especially to the Canons of Dort.

"We know very well," Schilder said, "that in the first years of the Secession there were many different opinions among the Seceded people."[18]

Cornelis Veenhof sketched the struggle concerning preaching and predestination in the church of the Secession between 1850 and 1870. There were at least two groups, the "Drenthe group" with the Rev. H. Joffers and the "Gelderland group" with Prof. A. Brummelkamp.[19]

For the sake of convenience we characterize these two nuances with the terms supralapsarian and infralapsarian.

(M. Th. thesis) (Grand Rapids, 1987). We should, however, never forget that Ten Hoor, defender of Secession principles, nevertheless joined the Union of 1892.

[18] K. Schilder, *De dogmatische beteekenis der "Afscheiding" ook voor onzen tijd* (Kampen: Kok, 1934) pp. 18, 21ff.

[19] C. Veenhof, *Prediking en uitverkiezing. Kort overzicht van de strijd, gevoerd in de Christelijk Afgescheidene Gereformeerde Kerk tussen 1850 en 1870, over de plaats van de leer der uitverkiezing in de prediking* (Kampen: Kok, 1959).

The "Drenthe group" was supralapsarian and the "Gelderland group" was infralapsarian. The infralapsarian view conformed better to the manner in which the Three Forms of Unity and the liturgical forms present the Reformed doctrine.

Who among the Secession theologians belonged to the infralapsarian movement with its confessional manner of presentation also with respect to covenant and baptism?

I mention the names of J. A. Wormser, A. Brummelkamp, K. J. Pieters, J. R. Kreulen, Helenius de Cock, W. H. Gispen and around 1905 L. Lindeboom, T. Bos, and the other signatories of the famous *Vijf stellingen* (Five Theses).

These Five Theses of 1905 were formulated by leaders who before 1892 had been members of the church of the Secession. They were directed against opinions of Abraham Kuyper c.s. and played a role in the doctrinal struggle that led to the Liberation of 1944.[20]

In this connection what is to be said about our American Secession theologians?

Well, first of all, there were nuances or differences of opinion also among them. The youngest one, Geerhardus

---

[20] C. Veenhof, *Prediking en uitverkiezing*; about Wormser and Brummelkamp pp. 159ff., Pieters and Kreulen pp. 61-66, Helenius de Cock chapter 5, pp. 88-131, Gispen p. 85, Lindeboom c.s. pp. 138f. Also about Wormser see id., *De Reformatie* 22:276ff., 284ff. For Brummelkamp is important M. te Velde, *Anthony Brummelkamp (1811-1888)* (Barneveld: De Vuurbaak, 1988). See further: *Vijf Stellingen betreffende leeringen, waarover in de Gereformeerde Kerken van Nederland in de laatste jaren verschil gevallen is. Aan de kerkeraden en voorts aan alle leden der gemeente ter overweging aangeboden door voorgangers en leden van genoemde kerken* (Five Theses regarding doctrines about which differences of opinion appeared in the Reformed Churches of the Netherlands these last few years. Presented to the consistories and members of the congregations for their consideration by leaders and members of above-mentioned churches) (Kampen: Kok, 1905). B. Holwerda wrote about the theologians of the Secession and 1905 in: R. J. Dam, B. Holwerda, and C. Veenhof, *Rondom "1905,"* pp. 31-68 (e.g. about L. J. Hulst, pp. 48-51). H. M. Yoo gives a survey about the debate between supralapsarian and infralapsarian theologians in the Netherlands during the last two centuries in *Raad en daad. Infra- en supralapsarisme in de nederlandse Gereformeerde theologie van de 19e en 20e eeuw* (Kampen: Dissertatie-uitgeverij Mondiss, 1990).

Vos, was a *supra*lapsarian thinker while the other six theologians were *infra*lapsarians.[21]

We distinguish them by speaking about the infralapsarian American Secession theologians — Hulst, Boer, Beuker, Hemkes, Ten Hoor, and Heyns — as "the six."

In their biographies we heard the names of Kreulen and Helenius de Cock. Kreulen influenced Hulst in what he called "my change in my view concerning the covenant."

Especially Helenius de Cock, the son of the father of the Secession, is important. After the Rev. T. F. de Haan he was the second professor of dogmatics in Kampen in the period from 1860 till 1882 when he was succeeded by Herman Bavinck. We saw that Hulst received his theological training in the pre-Kampen period but Helenius de Cock was the teacher of Beuker, Boer, Hemkes, Heyns, and Ten Hoor.[22]

There is also some influence of Herman Bavinck especially upon his class-mate Foppe Martin ten Hoor. Already Ten Hoor's definition of dogmatics reminds us of Bavinck: Dogmatics is the system of the knowledge of God which He in his Word has revealed to His church.[23]

---

[21] See Hulst and Hemkes, *Oud- en nieuw Calvinisme*, p. 62, about the influence of the supralapsarianism of G. Vos and his students. J. D. Bratt, *De erfenis van Kuyper in Noord-Amerika* (The inheritance of Kuyper in North America), in C. Augustijn a.o., eds., *Abraham Kuyper. Zijn volksdeel, zijn invloed* (his constituency, his influence) (Delft, 1987), p. 208 states that in America the Kuyperian ideas were championed by G. J. Vos and Ralph Janssen. Their work was clearly stamped by the master: supralapsarian. Among their infralapsarian adversaries were some pure Secession men — L. J. Hulst and H. van Hoogen — and some former opponents of Kuyper in the Netherlands who had emigrated to the United States, F. M. Ten Hoor and H. Beuker.

[22] C. Veenhof, *Prediking en uitverkiezing* ch. 5, deals with *Het onderwijs van Helenius de Cock* (The teaching of Helenius de Cock), pp. 88-131. It is characteristic for Helenius de Cock and his American pupils to make a clear distinction between Reformed doctrine and private opinions. See for his rejection of Kuyper's idea of presumed regeneration as the ground of baptism *De leer der wedergeboorte volgens de Gereformeerde Kerk* (The doctrine of regeneration according to the Reformed Church) (Kampen: J. H. Bos, 1892).

[23] *Dogmatiek is het systeem der kennis Gods, welke Hij in de H. Schrift aan Zijne kerk heeft geopenbaard, Compendium*, p. 5.

When we now try to sketch the insights of American Secession theologians concerning God's covenant of grace, we do so under the following sub-division:

1. Covenant and Election
2. Covenant and Christ
3. Covenant and Baptism

1. Covenant and Election

The title of the first sub-division, "covenant and election," implies the quest for a definition or description of the covenant. What is the character of the covenant of grace? Or as it is often called with the rather vague term: What is the *essence* of the covenant?

American Secession theologians, especially the six, made a definite distinction between God's covenant on the one hand and God's election and God's counsel of peace on the other hand.

God's election and God's covenant of redemption are *eternal* decrees, decrees from before the foundation of the world. God's covenant, however, is a relation established by God in the course of *time*.

Moreover, covenant and election are not identical. The number of God's elect is quantitatively not the same as the number of the members of God's covenant.

Hulst describes the difference in a simple and nevertheless very poignant and direct manner: "I read in some books of an *eternal covenant of grace*, established *by* God the Father *with* the Son, *about* the elect . . . . I wearied myself out to *find* the connection (the connection between God's eternal *decree* and the *execution* in the course of time, J.F.), and then I always ended up in the wrong direction: either I dominated with the decree the administration of reconciliation and became un-biblical and un-Reformed; or I dominated with the administration of reconciliation the decree of God and then I ended up in Arminian waters. But now I realized that no door is opened to us, men, to find this *connection* but the other way around that God had warned us to leave the hidden things to Him and to be satisfied with that which has been revealed, Deuteronomy 29:29 . . . .

When I saw this clearly, I abandoned that speculative idea of a covenant of grace from eternity and I descended to the covenant that God has established with *Abraham and his descendants*, Genesis 17. This is the covenant to which the entire Bible refers." This is clear language.[24]

Hulst, following Pieters, does not only refute the dogmatic construction of an eternal covenant of grace but he seems also to reject the concept of an eternal covenant of redemption or counsel of peace. He probably regarded it a scholastic speculation.[25]

Beuker, Ten Hoor, and Heyns, however, distinguish three covenants of God: the covenant of redemption or counsel of peace, the covenant of works, and the covenant of grace. At the same time they warn against an identification of covenant of redemption and covenant of grace.

Beuker states that the covenant of redemption and the covenant of grace differ in covenanting parties, covenant demands, and covenant promises.[26]

Heyns formulates that there is a difference as to the parties, as to the time of their being established, as to the character, and as to the purpose of both.[27]

---

[24] L. J. Hulst, *Drie en zestig jaren prediker*, pp. 57-60.

[25] Pieters wrote that the eternal connection of the three Persons to the idea of redemption was not discussed until the Scolasticism of the 17th century. See Hulst, *Supra en infra*, p. 43. Pieters refuted a.o. A. Comrie, Holtsius, and Brakel. On pp. 42-47 Hulst approvingly quotes K. J. Pieters, *Het baptisme, bij het licht der Schrift beoordeeld en in 't licht gesteld* ([Ana]baptism, assessed by the light of Scripture and brought in to the open) (Franeker, n.d. [1865?]), pp. 50f.

[26] H. Beuker, *Gereformeerde dogmatiek voor zijne leerlingen aan de Theologische school der Holl. Chr. Ger. Kerk in Grand Rapids* (Reformed Dogmatics for his students at the theological school of the Dutch Chr. Ref. Church), mimeographed class notes (1898?), p. 101, says *dat elke construeering van het genadeverbond niet anders, dan Infralapsarisch kan en mag gedacht worden* (that every constructing of the covenant of grace may not be considered from a different view than an Infralapsarian). See for the difference of the three covenants p. 104.

[27] W. Heyns, *Gereformeerde Geloofsleer (GG)*, p. 53; id., *Manual of Reformed Doctrine (Manual)* (Grand Rapids: Eerdmans, 1926), pp. 123-125 ("The Covenant of Grace to be distinguished from the Covenant of Redemption.") See further par. 254 in *GG* and *Manual*: "Identification of the Covenant of Grace and the Covenant of Redemption." Cf. also F. M. ten Hoor, *Compendium*, pp. 82-84.

There is a sort of contrast between Hulst, Beuker, Heyns, and Ten Hoor on the one hand and Geerhardus Vos on the other hand.

Whereas we heard clear language from Hulst, the exposition by Vos is ambiguous and inperspicuous.[28]

His definition of the covenant of grace is good: The covenant of grace "is the gracious alliance between the insulted God and the insulting sinner in which God promises salvation in the way of faith in Christ and the sinner accepts this in a believing manner."

Also Vos distinguishes the covenant of grace from the counsel of peace. One could ask a critical question when Vos is dealing with the connection between the two states: The counsel of peace is the eternal model (*het eeuwig voorbeeld*) of the temporal covenant of grace (94). But we should then acknowledge that, e.g., Beuker follows Vos when even he calls the counsel of peace "the eternal foundation and the perfect model" for the covenant of grace.[29]

More important is that Vos makes a distinction between the *external administration* of the covenant of grace and its *internal essence*: Everywhere . . . where there is not only the external administration of the covenant of grace but also its internal essence, this issues from the counsel of peace (95). Here we encounter the vague Dutch term *wezen*; the distinction is between *uitwendige bediening* (external administration) and *inwendig wezen* (internal essence). The question is whether this term *wezen* has to be translated by "essence" or by "substance."

Be this as it may, also Vos does not want to speak of an eternal covenant of grace. But when he asks the question: With whom is the covenant of grace in Christ established? the answer reads: The majority and the best of Reformed theologians answer: With the *elect* sinner (100). Even the vocabulary reminds us of Abraham Kuyper.

Vos speaks of two sides of the covenant (101) and says that the concept of covenant can be taken in a twofold sense.

---

[28] The numbers in the text refer to pages of Geerhardus Vos, *Dogmatiek*, Vol. 2, Anthropologie (Grand Rapids, 1910).

[29] H. Beuker, *Gereformeerde dogmatiek*, p. 104. Nevertheless, Beuker calls them "*wezenlijk verschillend*" (essentially different).

He makes a distinction that had an impact upon later Reformed theology in America, namely the distinction of covenant as alliance or agreement on the one hand and covenant as fellowship or communion on the other hand. In Dutch it is the distinction of *verbintenis* and *gemeenschap*. Agreement or alliance brings us into the legal or forensic sphere of *justice*, fellowship or communion into the sphere of *life*. There is covenant as *rechtsverbintenis* (judicial agreement) and covenant as *levensgemeenschap* (fellowship of life). The forensic agreement is also indicated as a being *under* the covenant and the fellowship of life as a being *in* the covenant. The purpose of the forensic agreement is the transition into the fellowship of life. Being *under* the covenant is meant to lead to a life *in* the covenant. Where the fellowship of life is absent, there the essence of the covenant is absent (106-109).

But this ambiguity obscures more than it illuminates.[30]

This ambiguity is also noticeable in Vos when he asks the question: What is the relationship between the covenant of grace and election?

His answer reads: As a covenant of communion, thus in its essence (*in zijn wezen*) it does not stretch further and is not broader than election. As a covenant agreement the covenant is wider than election (126).

When Geerhardus Vos thus restricts the being *in* the covenant to the elect only, he does not do full justice to the confessional expressions of Lord's Day 27 and of the Canons of Dort I, 17. We profess that infants as well as adults belong to God's covenant and congregation and that the children are holy, not by nature but in virtue of the covenant of grace, in which they are included with their parents.[31]

---

[30] The difference between G. Vos (and L. Berkhof) on the one side and W. Heyns and F. M. Ten Hoor on the other is neglected by C. Veenhof, *Predik het Woord* (Goes, n.d.), pp. 318f. and by A. A. Hoekema, "The Christian Reformed Church and the Covenant" in *Perspectives on the Christian Reformed Church* (Grand Rapids, 1983), pp. 185-201.

[31] See for the covenant view of his son, Johannes G. Vos, *The Covenant of Grace* (Pittsburgh, n.d.), p. 7, and these remarkable questions and answers: "2. When was the Covenant of Grace made? It was made in eternity, before the creation of the world, but it was not revealed to mankind until after Adam had broken the Covenant of Works . . . 5. Who are the parties in the Covenant of Grace? The parties are God, in the person of the Father, and the Lord Jesus Christ as the representative of elect sinners (those given Him by the Father, John 17:2)."

At the same time we must admit that especially Hulst and Hemkes but to a certain degree also Beuker and Heyns, with their right emphasis on God's establishing the covenant in the course of time, show a somewhat biblicist approach to the precise moment. They make a distinction between a promise of salvation *before* Abraham and a covenant of grace *with* Abraham. Hemkes, e.g., says that the believers who lived *before* Abraham, were saved *according* to the covenant God later established with Abraham and his descendants. But as yet the covenant of grace itself was not there.[32]

When one unduly stresses the difference between the promise of salvation *before* Abraham and the covenant of grace *with* Abraham, one forgets the truth of Bavinck's beautiful remark that covenant is the essence of religion. The true religion must always feature the figure of a covenant.[33]

Under this slight reservation one can accept Heyns's famous short definition: "Expressed very briefly, the covenant of grace is: the promise of salvation in the form of a covenant."[34] The covenant of grace, however, does not begin with Abraham; the promise of salvation in Genesis 3 already marks the transition of the covenant of God's favour into that of his grace.

We return to our comparison of Geerhardus Vos and "the six" and direct our attention to *Foppe Martin ten Hoor*.

Ten Hoor was influenced by Vos in his description of the covenant: The covenant of grace is the alliance between the

---

[32] G. K. Hemkes, *Onder of boven*, p. 9. Cf. L. J. Hulst, *Supra en infra*, pp. 42-47 (quoted in *De Reformatie* [*Ref.*], 19:370). See also H. Beuker, *De Gereformeerde Amerikaan (GA)*, 1:430/1 (*Ref.*, 19:339) and W. Heyns, *GA*, 4:60/1, 63, 180, 186 (*Ref.*, 19:348; 21:49), *Gereformeerde geloofsleer*, p. 127, *Manual*, par. 238 "The promise given in paradise and the covenant of grace" (cf. *Ref.*, 19, 347). Heyns *GA* 4:63 refers to H. Bavinck, *Gereformeerde dogmatiek* 1st ed., 3:193 (4th pr., Kampen: Kok, 1928, 3:183).

[33] H. Bavinck, *Gereformeerde dogmatiek* (Kampen: Kok, 1928), 1:279, 2:530, 531f., 3:184.

[34] W. Heyns, *Manual*, p. 125; *GG*, p. 126. See *Rapport. Breeder omschrijving van de gronden waarop het antwoord van de Christelijke Gereformeerde Kerk, Syn. 1934, aan De Gereformeerde Kerken rust* (Broader description of the grounds on which the answer of the [Dutch] Chr. Ref. Church Synod of 1934, to the Reformed Churches [in the Netherlands] is based), 3rd pr. (Dordrecht, 1938). This report refers to Hulst, Hemkes, and Heyns.

insulted God and the insulting but elect sinner, in which God promises salvation by way of faith in Christ, and the sinner accepts this in a believing manner.[35]

He also adopts a distinction similar to that of Vos between "legal relationship" and "fellowship of life" (*rechtsverbintenis* and *levensgemeenschap*, 122). Property does not yet mean possession. The distinction reminds us of that made later by J. G. Woelderink, the distinction between promise and fulfilment. But while Vos did not completely escape a dualism in his doctrine of the covenant, Ten Hoor not only rejects the distinction of an external and an internal covenant (148) but stresses that there is only *one* covenant of grace. Ten Hoor also emphatically states that the covenant as an historically existing institution of salvation embraces more than election, since according to Holy Scripture also the non-elect children of believers are within the covenant (132). His distinction of "legal relationship" and "fellowship of life" is a distinction of what the covenant as such is and what comes about within the covenant.[36]

Important in this connection is what Ten Hoor says about the essence of the covenant. The essence of the covenant cannot be situated in both the promise relationship and the communion of life. A covenant comes about by promises, through which two parties bind themselves to one another. The covenant does not come about only at the time of fulfilment of those promises. Having in mind this distinction of promise and fulfilment Ten Hoor comes to the formulation that the essence of the covenant of grace is the promise relationship (*belofteverbintenis*) and the goal is the appropriation of its gracious benefits through the Holy Spirit (180).

Ten Hoor thus calls the promise relationship or the legal bond the *essence* of the covenant and the communion of life its *purpose*. This goal, however, is not reached in all members of the covenant. Ten Hoor's distinction is a better one than

---

[35] Ten Hoor, *Compendium der Gereformeerde dogmatiek*, p. 121. The numbers in the text refer to this *Compendium*.

[36] Heyns uses the expression that the covenant of grace is wider than the circle in which it comes to its own (*tot zijn recht komt*), *GA*, 4:61 (cf. *Verhandelingen*, p. 40, *Ref.*, 19:348).

that of Vos who spoke of an external administration and an internal essence of the covenant.

At least the conclusion of our first sub-division on "covenant and election" may be that according to American Secession theologians covenant and election are not identical.

2. Covenant and Christ

Closely connected with the first doctrinal point is the second: covenant and Christ. In my opinion Geerhardus Vos is also in this respect ambiguous. He mentions the idea of those who regard the covenant of grace as a continuation of the counsel of peace. They speak of an eternal covenant of grace established with Christ as Head of the covenant. Vos says that Holy Scripture renders enough starting-points for this concept and refers then especially to Romans 5 and 1 Corinthians 15. He states that Paul in Romans 5 draws a parallel between Adam as head of the first and Christ as Head of the second covenant (97). We saw that Vos himself does not want to speak of an eternal covenant of grace but he maintains the expression "Christ as Head of the covenant" and he comes to the formulation that the covenant of grace is established with the elect sinner (100) in Christ as the Covenant Head (98).

Hulst, Beuker, Ten Hoor, and Heyns on the other hand make a clear distinction between the expression "Christ as Head *of* the covenant" and "Christ as Mediator *in* the covenant." As Geerhardus Vos they emphasize Christ's Mediatorship but they do not want to speak of Christ as "Head of the covenant."

Let us first listen to Ten Hoor in his *Compendium of Reformed dogmatics*. Nowhere in Holy Scripture — says Ten Hoor — is it taught that the covenant of grace is established with Christ as second party (138). Nowhere in Holy Scripture is Christ called Head of the covenant of grace. Since Christ is Surety and Mediator of the covenant, He cannot be the second party of it. Both concepts of Surety and Mediator presuppose the two parties of the covenant of grace. And these two parties are God and the sinner. Christ has been made sin but not a sinner and He cannot receive any grace. Ten Hoor says: One should not identify the covenant of grace with the covenant of redemption. Christ cannot be second party in a twofold capacity. In the capacity of second party in the covenant of redemption (covenant of works) He cannot be second party in the covenant of grace, and in the capacity of second party in the covenant of grace He cannot be second party in the covenant of peace (137).

Therefore, Ten Hoor states: Christ is the second party in the covenant of redemption but Christ is the first party in the covenant of grace together with the Father and the Holy Spirit.

Christ is also the central contents of all promises of the covenant. He can therefore not be the second party, for Christ cannot be given to Christ (139).

One could ask whether all Ten Hoor's arguments are valid. When he states that Christ cannot be party in a twofold capacity, does he not forget the distinction between the eternal Word before and after the incarnation, *Logos asarkos* and *Logos ensarkos*? The Son of God is the second Party in the covenant of redemption and Christ is the Mediator in the covenant of grace. But in the first relationship — the covenant of redemption — we speak of the Word who was with God and who is God; in the second — the covenant of grace — we deal with the Word become flesh, the Word that dwelt among us.

We also heard that Ten Hoor relates the position of Christ in the counsel of peace especially to the covenant of works.

In a similar vein *Heyns* states that while the covenant of works is established with a representing head of the covenant who decided for all, accepting or breaking the covenant of grace is a personal matter for any member of the covenant. The covenant of grace does not have a representing covenant head as the covenant of works had. Further, Christ is surely the organic Head of the covenant people that is His body but He is not the representing Head of the covenant itself. In the covenant of redemption He acted as representing Head. Scripture refers to this, when in Romans 5 it places Christ as Covenant Head over against Adam.[37]

---

[37] Cf. Heyns, *Manual*, pp. 71f. (*GG*, pp. 72f.) See also *Manual*, p. 124: "In the covenant of grace Christ is not the second Party over against the Father, but with the Father and the Holy Spirit He is the first party, over against us as second party." The original Dutch text added: Christ is representing Head of the covenant in the counsel of peace that is established with Him, but not Head in the covenant of grace that is established not with Him but by Him with Abraham and his descendants (*GG*, p. 125).

Here too the question arises whether the relation of the covenant of God's favour in paradise and the covenant of grace after the fall is pictured in the right manner and whether the unity of God's covenant with man in all its dispensations is maintained. Moreover, does Romans 5 speak about the covenant of redemption in eternity and does it indeed place Christ as covenant Head over against Adam? It is remarkable that Heyns left this sentence out in the later English edition. He maintained, however, that the covenant of grace does not have a representative Covenant-head.

Rightly so, for it is certainly good to abandon the concept of Christ as Head of the covenant of grace, as the six American Secession theologians did. It excludes any identification of covenant and eternal election or any confusion of God's covenant and His eternal counsel of peace.

Christ is not Head *of* the covenant but He is Head *in* the covenant. We profess in Canons of Dort I, 7 that God not only has chosen in Christ a definite number of persons but that He also from eternity appointed Christ to be the Mediator and Head of the elect and the foundation of salvation.

Let me summarize the insights of the six American Secession theologians on covenant and Christ as follows: The triune God established the covenant of grace with the believers and their children in Christ as Mediator of the covenant and Head of the elect. Although Christ is Mediator *in* the covenant, he is not the Head *of* the covenant.

3. Covenant and Baptism

The last doctrinal theme — covenant and baptism — brings us into well known territory. The infralapsarian American Secession theologians emphasize that *all* children of believers are children of the covenant and sanctified in Christ. The covenant promise of salvation is given to *all* these children. For *all* these children baptism is a sign and seal of the covenant of grace or that promise of salvation. As many of them who accept this promise by true faith, do so through the regenerating working of grace by the Holy Spirit, according to God's eternal election. The others are breakers of the covenant and they will be punished with a more severe punishment. Baptism is a seal of God's covenant promise and is not administered on the ground of presumed regeneration but on the basis of God's command.

It is the familiar language of the *Verklaring van gevoelen*, the Position Statement of the year 1943, preceding the Liberation in the Reformed Churches of the Netherlands. The concerned brothers, who objected against the doctrinal statements of General Synod 1942, gave in this Position Statement a positive exposition of their insights on covenant and baptism. They did so in conscious harmony with the teachings of Secession theologians as Pieters and Kreulen, Helenius de Cock and Lindeboom and we may add the names of the Americans Hulst, Beuker, Ten Hoor, and Heyns.

C. Veenhof, who was involved in the original draft of this Position Statement, states that the authors very consciously did not place covenant, promise, and baptism under the domination of God's eternal election. Further, they attempted to eliminate an objectivist tendency in the views of those Secession theologians.[38]

This last intriguing remark brings us back to one of the American Secession theologians, namely *William Wijnand Heyns.*

Heyns already tried to eliminate an objectivist tendency by elaborating on what he called "subjective Covenant-grace." Heyns was also especially interested in the question: What does it mean that covenant children are holy or sanctified in Christ?

Already in 1902 Heyns wrote an article in *De Gereformeerde Amerikaan* entitled *Iets over de subjectieve verbonds-genade* (remarks on subjective Covenant-grace). He inserted it later in the chapter on the benefits of the covenant in his lecture notes *Verhandelingen over het genade-verbond*, his Essays on the covenant of grace.[39]

Further, in 1903 Heyns occupied himself with the expression "sanctified in Christ." He did so in his *Liturgiek,*

---

[38] C. Veenhof, *Prediking en uitverkiezing*, p. 299.

[39] See for the concept of "subjective covenant-grace" *GA* (1902), 6:33-34, 171-172, 279-280, reprinted in *Verhandelingen over het genade-verbond*, pp. 70-75; further *Handboek voor de catechetiek*, pp. 141-146. Heyns treated the subject in section 248 of his dogmatic compendium *GG* or *Manual*, pp. 136f.

where he dealt with the beautiful and strong expressions from the Form for Baptism.

Heyns could not accept a merely objective explanation of this expression "sanctified in Christ" and spoke in this context of the most difficult question in the entire doctrine of the covenant.

In his Liturgics he also remarks that the whims of printers changed the original expression in the baptismal prayer "this *Thy* child" into the neutral words "this child." If one has followed a recent debate in *Nederlands Dagblad* and *Reformatorisch Dagblad*, a debate between what is now called the confessional Reformed group and the experiential Reformed group, one sees how timely the writings of an American Secession theologian can be![40]

Heyns writes in his *Handboek voor de catechetiek* (1907) about the ground of catechises. This ground is the covenant of grace and more precisely the fact that the children of the congregation are covenant children and that they participate in the covenant benefits. The catechism students are to be dealt with as members of the covenant. Heyns then posits a question that in his opinion cannot be avoided. It is the question about the subjective significance of the covenant for the catechism students.[41]

Heyns rejects Dr. Kuyper's *theologoumenon* of presumed regeneration at baptism. According to Kuyper, Christian nurture must start from the idea that there *is* the new life and it has only to be brought to its manifestation. But over against this Kuyperian view of covenant and baptism Heyns does not want to fall into a doctrine of presumed *non*-regeneration of covenant children. Often there is the idea of presumed *non*-regeneration, "if they — the children — have not abandoned all joyfulness of youth, in order to excel as examples of gloomy piety" (143).

---

[40] W. Heyns, *Liturgiek*, p. 204. The exposition on "sanctified in Christ" is to be found on pp. 208-210. Heyns refers a.o. to H. Bavinck, *Bazuin* 20:1900; *Heraut* No. 1168, 1170 and P. Biesterveld, *Het Gereformeerde kerkboek*, pp. 202ff.

[41] W. Heyns, *Handboek voor de catechetiek*, pp. 95-105. See about the subjective significance of the covenant for the catechism students (*de subjectieve beteekenis van het verbond voor de catechumenen*), pp. 144-146.

Searching the Scriptures Heyns found many proofs of God's *covenant grace* distinct from *saving grace*. Hulst and Heyns distinguished God's common grace, God's covenant grace, and God's saving grace. Already in his 1902 articles, later assembled in his Essays on the covenant of grace, he deals with "the subjective condition of the covenant member" and quotes the beautiful expressions about the union with Christ, about the children being received into grace in Christ, and the prayer that they may grow and increase in the Lord Jesus Christ. Heyns states that these expressions cannot be taken in a merely objective sense.[42]

Heyns is cautious. In his *Verhandelingen* he says that Scripture does not answer the question: What does this subjective grace specifically entail? The section in his *Manual of Reformed Doctrine* begins with the words "It seems to us . . .": "It seems to us that there is Scriptural evidence unmistakably pointing to an actual bestowal on the covenant members of a certain measure of subjective grace also, so that the subjective spiritual condition of the covenant children is different from that of the children outside of the covenant" (136).

Heyns' Scripture references are the following: In John 15 the unfruitful branches — covenant members — are branches "in Christ," organically united to him. Romans 11 designates the covenant members as branches which had become partakers of the root and the fatness of the olive tree. The Lord may rightfully ask of covenant members: What more could have been done to My vineyard that I have not done in it? Why then, when I expected it to bring forth good grapes, did it bring forth wild grapes? (Isaiah 5). These passages refer to a grace which does not insure salvation and yet takes from the covenant members all excuse.

Already in his earlier articles Heyns said that "a certain measure of life" in all covenant members cannot be denied. He quoted Acronius who in 1596 said that Christian nurture of covenant children was necessary, in order that they should not degenerate (*opdat zij niet veraerden*).[43] Parents, teachers,

---

[42] Heyns, *Verhandelingen*, p. 75.

[43] It is remarkable that Heyns, *Verhandelingen*, pp. 72, 74, quoted Acronius via the biased dissertation of a follower of A. Kuyper, namely

and ministers do not deal with "unfit material," with children who are completely blind and deaf spiritually, but with covenant children in whom the Lord has so worked that He may expect fruits of faith and repentance.

In his *Handboek voor de catechetiek* (1907) Heyns went so far as to speak of a subjective covenant grace for all members of the covenant so that man's total incapacity by nature for the things that are of the Spirit of God is taken away, that there is in the covenant child an initial or incipient capacity of covenantal nurture (145).

It is clear that Heyns tried to eliminate an objectivist feature and to do justice to the significance of baptism and of the position of the children of believers as sanctified in Christ and as heirs of God's kingdom and of His covenant. One may regret the fact that he did not escape the wrong dilemma of subjectivity and objectivity and in 1902 even fell into a speculation about a certain measure of spiritual life in all covenant children.

It is remarkable, however, that he did not repeat this speculation in his main works *Gereformeerde geloofsleer* of 1916 or *Manual of Reformed Doctrine* of 1926. In these works he again rejected supposed regeneration as the ground for baptism, since covenant and baptism are deprived of their objectivity. He also described "sanctified in Christ" positively as to mean that our children "are in the Covenant, and share in the benefits thereof, and also that they are for that reason members of the Church, and that they ought to bear the sign of the members of the Church" (*Manual*, 211).

Who will here quarrel with Heyns?

Let us end our second part on this positive confessional note: All children of believers are in the covenant and ought to bear the sign of baptism.

G. Kramer, *Het verband van doop en wedergeboorte* (The relationship of baptism and regeneration) (Breukelen, 1897), pp. 231, 233. He also quotes via Kramer an expression of Beza, namely that "subjective covenant grace can be shaken out (Dutch: *uitgeschud*) by unbelief." It is also remarkable that Heyns compares his idea of subjective grace in the Abrahamitic covenant with Kuyper's idea of the enhancing of common grace in the covenant with Noah, *Verhandelingen*, p. 83, *Manual*, p. 137. In my opinion both ideas are unacceptable.

III. INFLUENCE

We now come to the last part: the influence or impact of
the insights of the American Secession theologians. Let me
make some remarks about their influence on Louis Berkhof
and Herman Hoeksema on the American continent and on
Klaas Schilder in the Netherlands and about the interaction
between Hoeksema and Schilder.

Louis Berkhof
Louis Berkhof was Professor of Systematic Theology at
Calvin Theological Seminary from 1926 to 1944.

Berkhof taught that the covenant of grace is both
conditional and unconditional and he dedicated an entire
chapter to what he called "the dual aspect of the covenant." It
is clear that Berkhof followed the lead of Geerhardus Vos in
his preference for the distinction between the covenant as a
"legal relationship" and as a "fellowship of life." God
established the "legal relationship" with the believers and
their children, while the "fellowship of life" only includes the
elect. Berkhof states that the promises of God are given to the
seed of believers *collectively*, and not individually. On the
other hand, unregenerate persons are in the covenant *as far as*
their responsibility is concerned and in the sense that they
may lay claim to God's promises. Berkhof does not answer
the question how one may lay claim to promises that are not
given *individually*. As long as the children of the covenant do
not reveal the contrary, however, we shall, according to
Berkhof, have to proceed on the assumption that they are in
the possession of covenant life. Even unregenerate persons in
the covenant are subject to certain special operations and
influences of the Holy Spirit.[44]

In his essay on the "Christian Reformed Church and the
Covenant" Anthony Hoekema came to the conclusion that
Berkhof represents a mediating position, which avoids the
onesidedness of men like Kuyper and Van Lonkhuyzen, and
follows generally the position of Herman Bavinck, Vos,

---

[44] L. Berkhof, *Systematic Theology* (Grand Rapids: Eerdmans, 1938), pp.
280-281, 284-289. One finds a similar approach in W. Hendriksen, *The
Covenant of Grace* (Grand Rapids: Eerdmans, 1932).

Heyns, and Ten Hoor.[45] Although some expressions in Berkhof may be reminiscent of Heyns and ten Hoor, in my opinion we should not efface the difference between the supralapsarian position of Vos on the one hand and the infralapsarian approach to the covenant by Heyns and Ten Hoor on the other hand. In his chapter on "the dual aspect of the covenant" Berkhof followed especially Geerhardus Vos. Is what Anthony Hoekema called an avoidance of onesidedness in Louis Berkhof not a confusing ambiguity?

Herman Hoeksema

Herman Hoeksema as a supralapsarian theologian was influenced by Abraham Kuyper and his follower Geerhardus Vos. Although he rejected Kuyper's ideas of common grace, of baptismal grace, and of presupposed regeneration, he accepted his organism idea, his concept of the antithesis, and his definition of the essence of the covenant.

Hoeksema's doctrine of the covenant is dominated by his conception of God's double predestination. In the historical manifestation of the eternal covenant there is an elect kernel and a reprobate shell. There is an internal and an external covenant.

In his publication *Believers and Their Seed* Hoeksema defined God's covenant as "the living and eternal relation of friendship between Him and His elect people in Christ Jesus."[46] He stated in expressions that remind us of Geerhardus Vos: The reprobate are brought into "the sphere of the covenant" or live "under the covenant" (134). The essence of the covenant does not concern them. God's promise "is not for all who are born in the sphere of the historical manifestation of God's covenant" (21).

Right from the first chapter Hoeksema attacks the covenant conception of William Heyns "which has found

---

[45] A. A. Hoekema, "The Christian Reformed Church and the Covenant" in P. de Klerk and R. R. de Ridder, eds., *Perspectives on the Christian Reformed Church* (Grand Rapids, 1983), pp. 185-201, esp. p. 196.

[46] Herman Hoeksema, *Believers and Their Seed*, tr. Homer C. Hoeksema (Grand Rapids: Reformed Free Publishing Association, 1971), p. 133. The material was "first written in the Dutch language more than forty years ago" in *The Standard Bearer*. The original Dutch brochure *De geloovigen en hun zaad*, printed by C. J. Doorn, Grand Rapids, is without a date.

widespread acceptance and which, in our opinion, should be completely rooted out" (18). Rejecting his speculation about a certain subjective grace in all members of the covenant, Hoeksema characterizes Heyns' entire covenant conception by the title of the second chapter: "Arminianism injected into the Covenant." God "does not in the objective sense of the word bequeath (to use Prof. Heyns' language) upon all, head for head, His salvation and the benefits of the covenant" (21). To speak, as Heyns did, of a general covenant grace by which the members are put in a position to accept or to reject God's covenant, is "pure and simple Pelagianism applied to the area of God's covenant in the world . . . It is simply not true that God in holy baptism promises and seals something to all who are baptized" (139f.).

Hoeksema stated that the covenant conception of Heyns "has for years been imbibed by many who now serve as ministers in the Christian Reformed denomination." He regarded it as one of the main causes for the adoption by Synod 1924 of the doctrine of a general offer of grace on God's part in the preaching of the gospel. According to Hoeksema "the presentation of Prof. Heyns is nothing else than the old Pelagian error applied to the doctrine of the covenant" (20).

Hoeksema deals with Heyns' Scripture proofs for the concept of subjective covenant grace in the chapters "The organic idea in Scripture" and "The reprobate in the sphere of the covenant." In the one organism of God's people you have the elect kernel and the rejected shell. In Isaiah 5 the vineyard is addressed not from the viewpoint of the elect kernel but from that of the reprobate element. It is even the same when God in Psalm 80 speaks about "My people" that "did not listen to My voice." According to Hoeksema's hermeneutical historic-organic principle God speaks of "My people" not from the viewpoint of the spiritual nucleus but of the reprobate shell.

Also in John 15 the Saviour has in view His people as it manifests itself outwardly and Romans 11:17-21, too, deals with the covenant according to its outward form.

It is, however, remarkable that Hoeksema with respect to the reprobate shell acknowledges that there is "a certain influence of God's covenant" (136). One could even surmise some positive impact of Heyns' conception of the subjective significance of the covenant for all its members. Even Hoeksema assures that also the branches which are cast out, nevertheless "drew their life-sap out of that vine ... The branches which are cut out are not dead branches, which stand in no living connection with the vine whatsoever" (136).

By way of summary, it is clear that also Herman Hoeksema dealt with the legacy of the American Secession theologians. He forcefully rejected the infralapsarian approach of Hulst, Ten Hoor, and especially William Heyns and followed the lead of Geerhardus Vos whose supralapsarian position he even radicalized.

Klaas Schilder

In order to see the influence of the American Secession theologians in Klaas Schilder, let us in our imagination place ourselves in the year 1939. It was the year in which, in the providence of God, for the second time Dietrich Bonhoeffer came to America only to prematurely break off his visit because of the outbreak of the Second World War. It was the year in which Klaas Schilder, Professor of Dogmatics in Kampen in the Netherlands, sojourned in the United States for the first time. It was the year in which Dr. G. Ch. Aalders published his book about God's covenant.

Dr. Aalders was one of the deputies (1936) of the *Gereformeerde Kerken in Nederland* (GKN) for the investigation of opinions that deviated from the generally accepted teachings. It was the year in which Schilder in his weekly *de Reformatie* began discussing Aalders' book and prepared the minority report on the covenant of grace for the up-coming Synod of Sneek 1939.

Aalders had written that *the* covenant of grace is established with Christ and in Him with all those who are included in Him. "There can therefore be no doubt that the elect are the participants in the covenant of grace. Covenant and election are quantitatively identical; the number of the covenant members is equal to that of the elect." Christ is, according to Aalders, the Head of the covenant of grace.[47]

---

[47] G. Ch. Aalders, *Het verbond Gods* (The Covenant of God) (Kampen, 1939), p. 193.

During his journey in the spring of 1939 Schilder became re-acquainted with the American Secession theologians. He visited Geerhardus Vos whose principal's address after almost half a century was being reprinted in Rotterdam. After his series "Impressions of my journey" and a series of articles about the schism in America — the so-called Hoeksema case — Schilder started a long series of articles about God's covenant. He refuted Aalders' idea that covenant and election are identical. He quoted at length the publications of American Secession theologians. Schilder had discovered, or rediscovered, *De Gereformeerde Amerikaan*. Hulst, Ten Hoor, Beuker, and especially Heyns reappeared on the theological scene of the Netherlands.[48]

Remarkable is Schilder's emphasis on the distinction of Christ as Head of the elect and as Mediator of the covenant of grace. He denies that Christ is Head *of* the covenant of grace. But another Dutch weekly — *Calvinistisch Weekblad* — avers that Schilder turned his coat and it quotes a remark Schilder had made in 1929 in which he seemed to defend the idea of Christ as representing Head of the covenant of grace. Schilder took pains to show that he was still wearing the same coat. Nevertheless, he did not deny that there had been a development in his thinking about God's covenant. He wrote that the argumentation by Dr. S. Greijdanus about the ground of the imputation of Adam's sin had made him think differently about Romans 5. Now in 1939 Aalders had neglected the issue of the prepositions "with" and "in." Is the covenant of grace established *with* Christ or *in* Christ? Schilder states: "The group of older theologians I mentioned (that is the group of American Secession theologians, J.F.) had authors with sharper sense of distinctions."[49]

So there had not only been the influence of Greijdanus but also of the Secession theologians Beuker, Ten Hoor, and Heyns whom Schilder had studied more intensively during

---

[48] K. Schilder, *Ref.*, 19:315ff. (Vos), 322f. (Hulst, Heyns, Ten Hoor), 330f. (Ten Hoor, Hulst), 338f. (Beuker), 346f. (Heyns), 357 (Heyns), 362ff. (Heyns), 370 (Hulst).

[49] *Ref.*, 19:402. Cf. J. Faber, "Prof. Dr. S. Greijdanus als dogmaticus," *Almanak Fides Quaerit Intellectum* (Kampen, 1948), 54:99-184, esp. pp. 107-112.

his American trip in this year of 1939. They provided ammunition in the theological battle in which Schilder saw even his ecclesiastical position endangered.

After the Second World War, and after the political and ecclesiastical liberation, Schilder published a series of articles entitled "Unanimity on the covenant of grace?" This series in the first volume of the renewed weekly *De Reformatie* must have been the material of his minority report for the synod of Sneek-Utrecht 1939-1942. In these articles Schilder deals with the question whether there had been generally accepted teachings on God's covenant in the Reformed Churches or not. He answers this question with "No." Beside the teachings of Abraham Kuyper c.s. there had been the teachings of Hulst and Hemkes, of Beuker and Heyns. Schilder again gives lengthy quotations of American Secession theologians to show that there was no unanimity among Reformed theologians on important points of doctrine concerning the covenant of grace.[50]

Here we see again the significance and the impact of the insights of American Secession theologians on covenant and baptism.

Interaction between Hoeksema and Schilder

In 1947, during his second American journey, Schilder was officially refused entry onto Christian Reformed pulpits.

When the Protestant Reformed Churches — the so called Hoeksema group — opened their doors to him, Schilder did his utmost to remove theological misunderstandings between Hoeksema c.s. and the churches that in the Liberation had remained truly Reformed. He was concerned for the Dutch emigrants who began to stream to the United States and Canada. When in the Protestant Reformed Churches Schilderianism was being equated with Heynsianism and Heynsianism with Arminianism, Schilder was confronted with a quotation of Heyns' *Catechetiek*. In the train that brought him back from California to Michigan Schilder penned an article that did not do complete justice to William

---

[50] *Ref.*, 21:41ff., 49f. (Hulst and Hemkes, Vos, Heyns), 57f. (Heyns, Hulst, Hemkes).

Heyns. In his ecumenical zeal Schilder went too far when he wrote about the utterly wrong paths of Heyns and argued that Heyns, in his statements about "subjective Covenant-grace" sympathized with the Arminians.

In 1939 Schilder had acknowledged terminological weaknesses in the American Secession theologians. Then he pointed, e.g., to their predilection of the expression that the covenant of grace is *monopleuric*, one-sided. Schilder preferred the formulation that the covenant is monopleuric (one-sided) in its origin and *dipleuric* (two-sided) in its existence.

We mention in this context that also Heyns' *Essays* began with three sections on the character of God's covenant. They picture the covenant as first monopleuric, then unbreakable, and third unconditional.[51] This is no Arminianism at all! Just the other way around, here are terminological weaknesses of a brother who otherwise certainly acknowledged human responsibility.

Heyns writes: "Even in the Covenant of Works the condition of obedience was not a condition for being taken into the Covenant, but for keeping the Covenant and for gaining its reward. In the same way faith and obedience are conditions for keeping the Covenant of Grace and for inheriting the promise, Heb. 6:15, whereas unbelief and disobedience make the Covenant member a Covenant breaker, who shall not enter in, Heb. 3:18-19." If in the so-called covenant of works obedience was no condition for being taken into the covenant, then certainly it was, according to Heyns, no condition for being taken into the covenant of grace. This is precisely the opposite of the Arminian doctrine of the covenant.

Not only in this exposition but also when he in his *Manual* preferred to call faith and obedience no conditions but obligations of the covenant, Heyns showed how perceptible he was to the danger of Arminianism.[52]

---

[51] W. Heyns, *Verhandelingen*, pp. 7-12 (*monopleurisch*), pp. 13-15 (*onverbrekelijk*), pp. 16-19 (*onvoorwaardelijk*). Idem, sections 240-243 in *GG* and *Manual*.

[52] W. Heyns, *Manual*, p. 131. Herman Hoeksema neglected these passages when he characterized Heyns' covenant conception as a "conditional relationship in which God places Himself to the seed of the covenant, the

But he struggled against the teaching of presumed regeneration and at the same time he desired to do full justice to covenant and baptism, to the liturgical expression "sanctified in Christ" and above all to Scriptural data. He writes then about "subjective Covenant-grace." He may be weak terminologically and even theologically, especially in certain statements in his *Catechetiek*, but in Heyns' entire theological work it was only a detail and we should not immediately conjure up the bogeyman of Arminianism. I do not know of any Catechetics in which the Reformed doctrine of the covenant of grace is as central as in that of Heyns.

Heyns tried to distinguish between common grace, covenant grace, and saving grace. He was in line with Hulst and one could even think of distinctions made by earlier Reformed theologians such as Van Mastricht and a Marck. They had distinguished between universal grace, common grace, and saving grace (*gratia universalis, gratia communis*, and *gratia salutaris*).[53] The point now is not whether these distinctions are valid or helpful but whether their use as such betrays influence of Arminianism. If one reads all their expositions, one must say that Van Mastricht and a Marck did not sympathize with the Arminians and neither did Hulst or Heyns.

Heyns fought against the teachings of both presumed regeneration and presumed *non*-regeneration. Alas, he did not overcome the dilemma of subjectivism and objectivism. American Secession theologians were weak not only terminologically but also philosophically. They had not yet studied Vollenhoven's philosophy of cosmonomic idea. Heyns also had a lack of insight in the *forensic* character of the in-being of covenant members as branches *in* Christ.

---

realization of which depends on the consent and acceptance of the covenant-member," *Believers and Their Seed*, tr. Homer C. Hoeksema (Grand Rapids: Reformed Free Publishing Association, 1971), p. 22 in the chapter entitled "Arminianism injected into the covenant."

[53] Cf. H. Kuiper, *Calvin on Common Grace* (Goes: Oosterbaan & Le Cointre, 1928), Appendix. In a discussion of Romans 6:3, 4 Hulst makes a distinction between *algemeene genade, verbondsgenade*, and *zaligmakende genade* and states that in the middle sphere one has nothing to do with God's decree, *Drie en zestig jaren prediker*, p. 60.

If one has to use a sticker, I would say that although he rejected Kuyper's idea of a special baptismal grace, Heyns' concept of subjective Covenant-grace was — in line with Kuyper — a Romanizing speculation about internal, infused, or preparatory grace (*gratia interna* or *gratia infusa* or *gratia praeparans*). The only difference is that Kuyper thought of Christ as dispensing special infused grace during the act of baptism while Heyns speculated about God granting special internal grace in establishing the covenant.[54]

Let us in the meantime not forget that Heyns wanted to listen to Holy Scripture in, e.g., Isaiah 5, John 15, and Romans 11. One could add references to texts from Hebrews 6 and Hebrews 10, where Scripture speaks about apostate members of God's covenant "who have once been enlightened, who have tasted the heavenly gift, and have become partakers of the Holy Spirit and have tasted the goodness of the Word of God and the powers of the age to come" (6:4, 5). Such a covenant child "has spurned the Son of God, and profaned the blood of the covenant by which he was sanctified, and outraged the Spirit of grace" (10:29). Such texts should remain operative in our doctrine of God's covenant and baptism.

Precisely in connection with the passage of Isaiah 5 Heyns rejects Pelagianism. He writes in his *Manual* that it would be Pelagian doctrine if this passage would mean that on account of merely external work the Lord had full right to expect good fruit. He adds that the grace referred to is not a grace which insures salvation. It is not a grace which as such renders the covenant member capable of faith and repentance. It is a grace which takes from him or her all excuse for not bringing forth the desired fruit of the covenant.[55]

---

[54] Heyns rejected not only Kuyper's idea of presumed regeneration as the ground of baptism but also his speculation about a special operation of Christ in baptism by which the implanted faith is set into fellowship with the body of Christ, A. Kuyper, *E Voto* (Kampen, Kok, n.d. [1892?]), 2:535, 544. Heyns called it a "certain magical operation," *Verhandelingen*, p. 62. In America the idea was spread by J. Van Lonkhuyzen, *Heilig zaad*, pp. 43-51. A good summary is found in H. Hoeksema, *Believers and Their Seed*, pp. 34ff.

[55] Heyns, *Manual*, pp. 136f.; *Verhandelingen*, p. 83.

Alas, Schilder did not sufficiently acknowledge Heyns' intention in his *Catechetiek* and therefore he did not do full justice to this American Secession theologian. Moreover, Heyns' articles about "subjective Covenant-grace" had already been published in *De Gereformeerde Amerikaan* in 1902. His *Liturgiek* was of 1903 and his *Handboek voor de catechetiek* of 1907. As far as I know, Heyns' insights never became objects of special attention or an ecclesiastical *gravamen* by Hoeksema c.s. or by anyone else for that matter.

Therefore, also for this reason Schilder in 1947 should and could have more strongly defended his seceded brother Heyns over against Hoeksema's supralapsarianism. After the synod of Sneek-Utrecht and its aftermath precisely Schilder could know that the accusation of Arminianism is sometimes made too hastily and then continues to resound for too long a period.

But it should be said in Schilder's honour: When after his second American journey the Protestant Reformed Churches drafted the infamous *Declaration of Principles* (1950), K. Schilder was immediately alert. He had rejected the dilemma of supralapsarianism and infralapsarianism in line with what he called the most beautiful pages of Bavinck's Dogmatics. In an illicit manner the dilemma carries the element of *chronos* (time), and thus of chronology, into the doctrine of God's *eternal* decrees. But Schilder never neglected the Scriptural intention of infralapsarianism. It shows up in his teaching about God's creation, about God's covenant, and about God seriously offering *Christ* in the gospel and sincerely offering the *gospel* in Christ. God's acts in history — creation, covenant, and the gospel proclamation — are not only means to another goal but have significance in themselves.[56]

Over against Hoeksema Schilder remained faithful to the Act of Liberation and, though he was painfully hurt, he consciously maintained his struggle against extra-Scriptural binding.

---

[56] Cf. K. Schilder, *Heidelbergsche Catechismus* (Goes, 1949), Vol. 2, par. 46, *De Middelaar "aangeboden"* (the Mediator "offered"), pp. 237-260; id. (Goes, 1950), Vol. 3, par. 71, *De schepping als acte van vroolijke, spontane besluitvaardigheid*, pp. 453-480.

Then in his last discussion with Hoeksema Schilder rightly writes: "No more than Kuyper should become a bogey or legend in the Netherlands, Heyns should become such in America."[57]

The kinship of the fifth dogmatician of Kampen with the American Secession theologians, also with Heyns, came out.[58]

CONCLUSION

What is our situation with respect to the doctrine of God's covenant and baptism today?

In 1980 Fred H. Klooster commented that in recent years the Reformed community has generally not been in the forefront of studies regarding God's covenant. "Fear of new divisions, embarrassment with past separations, and a general lethargy appear to have contributed to the neglect of the covenant doctrines by many within the Reformed churches." Also, in 1983, Anthony A. Hoekema noted that this doctrine is not as prominent in the theological reflection of the Christian Reformed Church as it once was.[59]

---

[57] K. Schilder, *Ref.*, 26:66. Cf. *Bovenschriftuurlijke binding - een nieuw gevaar* (extra-Scriptural binding — a new danger) (Goes n.d.), p. 28. In a short entry about Heyns in the second edition of *Christelijke Encyclopedie* 3:459, F. L. Bos states that Heyns did not completely escape the reproach of Arminian deviation. In my opinion it was only a minimal point and even if one disagrees with Heyns on this point, the blame of deviation into Arminianism should not be voiced anymore. In his Preface Prof. H. Bouwman of Kampen rightly characterized Heyns' *Gereformeerde geloofsleer* (1916) as "soundly Reformed" (*gezond Gereformeerd*).

[58] At the end of 1951, half a year before his death, Schilder wrote a famous article *De kous is af* (the stocking is finished) in which he takes leave of his friend Hoeksema c.s., *Ref.*, 27:61-63. An English translation and parts of Hoeksema's answer are to be found in R. van Reest, *Schilder's Struggle for the Unity of the Church*, tr. T. Plantinga (Neerlandia: Inheritance Publications, 1990), pp. 433-444.

[59] F. H. Klooster, "Covenant Theology Today," *The Messenger* 51:6-9 (January 1980) quoted by A. A. Hoekema in De Klerk and De Ridder (eds.), *Perspectives on the Christian Reformed Church*, p. 199.

Who should not weep? And what about the future?

Let us not fall into an unhealthy silence. On our American continent there is still a role to be played by the Secession theologians. We are now engaged in a captivating process. The dynamics of Christ gathering His catholic church is always breathtaking but especially in our situation. The rise of Independent Christian Reformed Churches and the formation of the Alliance of Reformed Churches brought renewed contacts between Reformed confessors on this American continent. For a part they too have their roots in the Secession in the Netherlands of 1834. There is movement in and between the Free Reformed, the Independent Christian Reformed and the Canadian Reformed Churches.

Twenty-five years ago "Hamilton" was established to maintain and strengthen the ecclesiastical unity of Reformed confessors in Canada and the United States and if it pleases God, to restore this unity where it has been broken. It also means: We know that we stand in a good tradition of Kampen, Apeldoorn, and Grand Rapids. It is the tradition of Brummelkamp and Helenius de Cock, of Lindeboom and Wielenga, of Greijdanus, Schilder, and Veenhof, and with a view to our Free Reformed brothers and sisters I do not hesitate to add, the tradition of Van der Schuit, Van der Meiden, and Hovius, to mention only a few of those who passed the Jordan of death. As far as Grand Rapids is concerned, it is the tradition of especially Beuker, Ten Hoor, and Heyns and also of Vos, cleared from ambiguities. It is the tradition of Reformed and therefore confessionally determined, covenantal theology.

At the end of this twentieth century the *confessional* unity of Reformed confessors ought to find an *ecclesiastical* manifestation according to the demand of God and the prayer of Christ. On our American continent there is a gripping secularisation. Sure, sometimes there seems to be much old-fashioned piety but often this is no more than religious individualism. There are still those who adhere to the Three Forms of Unity. They still use the liturgical Forms for Baptism and the Lord's Supper from the time of the Reformation in the Pfaltz and the Netherlands. They have such a tremendous common heritage with respect to the Reformed understanding of God's covenant and baptism. Let them unite!

When I was young, we sang Psalm 25 about *hen die Gods verbond en woorden als hun schatten gadeslaan* (those who keep God's covenant and words as their treasures). We should regard God's covenant and baptism as our treasures, also theologically and ecclesiastically, and we should do so *together*. At the same time we should remember that Christ is not gathering a church of theologians or church historians, but of *believers*.

This is the *kairos*, the specific moment, at the end of this twentieth century, after 140 years Kampen, 50 years Liberation, and 25 years Hamilton.

Let "Hamilton," its professors, its former and present students, continue working in the confessional and therefore non-sectarian line of Secession, Union, and Liberation. God's catholic church is being gathered, not in the unity of a perfect theology — however eagerly we should endeavour to obtain it — but in the unity of true faith, faith in the triune God of the covenant, the God of our baptism.

Hamilton, Ontario   J. Faber

Extra-Scriptural Binding

—

A New Danger

A Collection of Articles
by
Professor Dr. K. Schilder
published in
de Reformatie
during 1950-51
in connection with the
Declaration of Principles
of the
Protestant Reformed Churches

Translated by T. vanLaar

The following is a translation of a series of articles that appeared in the weekly *De Reformatie* in the Netherlands in response to the Declaration of Principles written by the Mission Committee of the Protestant Reformed Churches and to articles written by Professor Herman Hoeksema. Many of the immigrants from the Netherlands to Canada and the U.S.A. were advised by Dr. Klaas Schilder to seek membership in the Protestant Reformed Churches, but were deterred from doing so by the *Declaration of Principles*.

Chapter 1
Occasion and Reason

In the Protestant Reformed Churches in the United States of North America a *Brief Declaration* concerning various points of doctrine was presented to a general synod. The intention was that this synod should approve this document and propose it to the churches, with the purpose of accepting it as final at the next general synod should the churches approve.

The above mentioned synod set its seal of *provisional* approval on this *Brief Declaration*. It decided to send it to the churches along with the stated intention, adding that in the meantime it should be used as a "working hypothesis." Meanwhile some difficulties arose concerning this *Brief Declaration*. Many new immigrants could not accept it as binding. When a classis declared that those who wished to join a Protestant Reformed Church would have to submit to instruction in the Protestant Reformed doctrine (as it was stated in this declaration) and would have to promise not to teach anything that contradicted the Protestant Reformed theology the difficulties quickly increased.

This development moved the present writer to begin a discussion on this *Brief Declaration* in *de Reformatie*. Such a discussion was also requested by others. The fact that exactly at this time the possibility of church correspondence with the Protestant Reformed Churches[1] is being considered, made a discussion in the press even more desirable.

One could remark that this declaration is only the business of the Protestant Reformed Churches and that Dutch readers should keep out of it. However, it appears that Dutch readers

---

[1] Schilder was a member of the Reformed Churches in the Netherlands (liberated). — Ed.

are also following this discussion with interest, for it touches to some extent upon the points which in 1944 created so much trouble in our country. Although colleague Hoeksema (Grand Rapids, supporter of the *Brief Declaration*) openly resisted the imposed binding to the formulas of 1942-1944, and although he was vehemently opposed to the church polity then "introduced" (or at least, used), he nevertheless thought that something in this *Brief Declaration* would acknowledge his objections against the synodical actions of 1944 (in the Netherlands), while remaining faithful to the confession.

For that reason, and also on request of Dutch readers, you find in this booklet a (slightly revised) reprint of the articles of *de Reformatie*.

First we give the text of the *Brief Declaration* (the parts that are relevant).[2] The text is as follows:

A BRIEF DECLARATION OF PRINCIPLES
OF THE
PROTESTANT REFORMED CHURCHES

{DECLARATION OF PRINCIPLES, *to be used only by the Mission Committee and the missionaries for the organization of prospective churches on the basis of Scripture and the Confessions as these have always been maintained in the Protestant Reformed Churches and as these are now further explained in regard to certain principles.*}

---

[2] Schilder published a complete translation (translated by Prof. Herman Hoeksema) of the provisionally adopted text (by the Protestant Reformed Synod of 1950) of the *Declaration*. He only left out the bulk of the quotes from the Three Forms of Unity, which he substituted with "(was quoted)," etc. We reproduce the original English text, in the same manner as Schilder published the translation. In the final text of the *Declaration* adopted by the Protestant Reformed Synod of 1951 some changes were made (which we reproduce in between { }). Many more proof texts from the Three Forms of Unity, and the Form for the Administration of Baptism were also added. We will restrict ourselves to only mentioning the references. All clarifications, comments, etc. of the editor are set in [ ] and/or in footnotes. The reader should keep in mind that the text used for the Forms is from The Psalter (Grand Rapids: Wm. B. Eerdmans, 1927). — Ed.

The Protestant Reformed Churches stand on the basis of Scripture as the infallible Word of God and of the Three Forms of Unity. Moreover, they accept the Liturgical Forms used in the public worship of our churches, such as the Baptism Form *et alii*, as confessions of minor order.

{. . . such as:

Form for the Administration of Baptism, Form for the Administration of the Lord's Supper, Form of Excommunication, Form of Readmitting Excommunicated Persons, Form of Ordination of the Ministers of God's Word, Form of Ordination of Elders and Deacons, Form for the Installation of Professors of Theology, Form of Ordination of Missionaries, Form for the Confirmation of Marriage before the Church, and the Formula of Subscription.}

On the basis of this Word of God and these confessions:

I. They repudiate the errors of the Three Points adopted by the Synod of the Christian Reformed Church of Kalamazoo, 1924, which maintain:

A. That there is a grace of God to all men, including the reprobate, manifest in the common gifts to all men.

B. That the promise {. . . the preaching} of the gospel is a gracious offer of salvation on the part of God to all that externally hear the gospel.

C. That the natural man through the influence of common grace can do good in this world.

D. Over against this they maintain:

1. That the grace of God is always particular, i.e., only for the elect, never for the reprobate.

2. That the promise {. . . the preaching} of the gospel is not a gracious offer of salvation on the part of God to all men, nor a conditional offer to all that are born in the historical dispensation of the covenant, that is, to all that are baptized, but an oath of God that He will infallibly

lead all the elect unto salvation and eternal glory through faith.

3. That the unregenerate man is totally incapable of doing any good, wholly depraved, and therefore can only sin.

{For proof we refer to Canons [of Dort] I, A, 6-8; Canons II, A, 5 [quoted in full in 1951 edition, as are all following references];

The Canons in II, 5 speak of the preaching of the promise. It presents the promise, not as general, but as particular, i.e., as for believers, and, therefore, for the elect. This *preaching* of the particular promise is promiscuous to all that hear the gospel with the *command*, not a condition, to repent and believe.

Canons II, B, 6 [B = Rejection of Errors];

For further proof we refer to the Heidelberg Catechism III, 8 and XXXIII, 91;

And also from the Netherlands [= Belgic] Confession, Art. XIV;

Once more we refer to Canons III and IV, A, 1-4;}

II. They teach on the basis of the same confessions:
   A. That election, which is the unconditional and unchangeable decree of God to redeem in Christ a certain number of persons, is the sole cause and fountain of all our salvation, whence flow all the gifts of grace, including faith. This is the

plain teaching of our confessions in the Canons of Dordrecht, I, A, 6, 7 (they are quoted).

And in the Heidelberg Catechism, XXI, Qu. and A. 54, we read: (it is quoted).

This is also evident from the doctrinal part of the Form for the Administration of Baptism, where we read: "For when we are baptized . . . among the assembly of the elect in life eternal."

B. That Christ died only for the elect and that the saving efficacy of the death of Christ extends to them only. This is evident from the Canons of Dordrecht, II, A, 8: (quotation follows).

This article very clearly teaches:

1. That all the covenant blessings are for the elect alone.
2. That God's promise is unconditionally for them only: for God cannot promise what was not objectively merited by Christ.
3. That the promise of God bestows the objective right of salvation not upon all the children that are born under the historical dispensation of the covenant, that is, not upon all that are baptized, but only upon the spiritual seed.

    This is also evident from other parts of our confessions, as for instance:

    Heidelberg Catechism, {XXV} Qu. 65 {and 66}: "Since then we are made partakers of Christ and all His benefits by faith only, whence doth this faith proceed? From the Holy Ghost, who works faith in our hearts by the preaching of the gospel, and confirms it by the use of the sacraments."

And in Qu. 66 we read: "What are the sacraments?" "The sacraments are holy visible signs and seals, appointed of God for this end, that by the use thereof, he may the more fully declare and seal to us the promise of the gospel, viz., that he grants us freely the remission of sin, and life eternal, for the sake of that one sacrifice of Christ, accomplished on the cross."

If we compare with these statements from the Heidelberger what was taught concerning the saving efficacy of the death of Christ in Canons II, A, 8, it is evident that the promise of the gospel which is sealed by the sacraments concerns only the believers, that is, the elect.

This is also evident from Heidelberg Catechism {XXVII} Qu. 74 (quotation follows in the original).

That in this question and answer of the Heidelberger not all the children that are baptized, but only the spiritual children, that is, the elect, are meant is evident. For:

{a.} 1. Little infants surely cannot fulfill any conditions. And if the promise of God is for them, the promise is infallible and unconditional and therefore only for the elect.
{b.} 2. According to Canons II, A, 8, which we quoted above, the saving efficacy of the death of Christ is for the elect alone.
{c.} 3. According to this answer of the Heidelberg Catechism, the Holy Ghost, the author of faith, is promised to the little children no less than to the adult. And God surely fulfills His promise. Hence, that promise is surely only for the elect.

The same is taught in the Netherlands Confession, Articles 33 - 35. In Article 33 we read:

"We believe, that our gracious God . . . without whom they would be of no moment."[3]

And from Article 34, which speaks of Holy Baptism, we quote:

"We believe and confess that Jesus Christ, who is the end of the law . . . and putting off the old man with all his deeds."

{Article XXXIV speaks of holy baptism.} That all this, washing and cleansing and purging our souls of all filth and unrighteousness, the renewal of our hearts, is only the fruit of the saving efficacy of the death of Christ and therefore is only for the elect is very evident. The same is true of what we read in the same article concerning the baptism of infants:

{Art. XXXIV.} "And indeed Christ shed his blood no less for the washing of the children of the faithful, than for adult persons. And therefore they ought to receive the sign and sacrament of that which Christ has done for them. As the Lord commanded in the law that they should be made partakers of the sacrament of Christ's suffering and death shortly after they were born by offering for them a lamb, which was a sacrament of Jesus Christ. Moreover, what circumcision was to the Jews that baptism is to our children. And for this reason Paul calls baptism the circumcision of Christ."

If, according to Article 8 of the Second Head of Doctrine, A, in the Canons, the saving efficacy of the death of Christ extends only to the elect it follows that when in this article of the Netherlands Confession it is stated that "Christ shed his blood no less for the washing of the children of the faithful than for the adult persons" also here the reference is only to the elect children.

---

[3] A more recent translation of Art. 33 has "apart from Him [Jesus Christ] they would be nothing." — Ed.

Moreover, that the promise of the gospel which God signifies and seals in the sacraments is not for all is also abundantly evident from Article 35 of the same Netherlands Confession, which speaks of the Holy Supper of our Lord Jesus Christ. For there we read:

{Art. XXXV.} "We believe and confess, that our Savior Jesus Christ did ordain and institute the sacrament of the holy supper, to nourish and support those whom he hath already regenerated, and incorporated into his family, which is his Church."

In the same article we read: "Further, though the sacraments are connected with the thing signified, nevertheless both are not received by all men: the ungodly indeed receives the sacrament to his condemnation, but he does not receive the truth of the sacrament. As Judas, and Simon the Sorcerer, both indeed received the sacrament, but not Christ, who was signified by it, of whom believers only are made partakers."

It follows from this that both the sacraments as well as the preaching of the gospel are a savor of death unto death for the reprobate as well as a savor of life unto life for the elect. Hence, the promise of God preached by the gospel signified and sealed in both the sacraments is not for all, but for the elect only.

And that the election of God, and consequently the efficacy of the death of Christ and the promise of the gospel, is not conditional is abundantly evident from the following articles of the Canons:

Canons I, A, 10: "The good pleasure of God is the sole cause of this gracious election; which does not consist herein, that out of all possible qualities and actions of men God has chosen some as a condition of salvation; but that he was pleased out of the common mass of sinners to adopt some certain persons as a peculiar people to himself, as it is written, 'For the children not yet born neither having done any good or evil,' etc. it was said (namely to Rebecca): 'the elder shall serve the younger; as it is written, Jacob have I loved, but Esau have I hated.' Romans 9:11, 12, 13. 'And as many as were ordained to eternal life believed.' " Acts 13:48.

In Canons I, B, 2, the errors are repudiated of those who teach:

{Art. 2.} "That there are various kinds of election of God unto eternal life: the one general and indefinite, the other particular and definite. And that the latter in turn is either incomplete, revocable, non decisive and conditional, or complete, irrevocable, decisive and absolute . . ."

And in the same chapter of Canons I, B, 3, the errors are repudiated of those who teach:

{Art. 3.} "That the good pleasure and purpose of God, of which the Scripture makes mention in the doctrine of election, does not consist in this, that God chose certain persons rather than others, but in this that he chose out of all possible conditions (among which are also the works of the law), or out of the whole order of things, the act of faith which from its very nature is undeserving as well as its incomplete obedience, as a condition of salvation, and that he would graciously consider this in itself as a complete obedience and count it worthy of the reward of eternal life . . ."

Again in the same chapter of Canons I, B, 5, the errors are rejected of those who teach that:

{Art. 5.} ". . . faith, the obedience of faith, holiness, godliness and perseverance are not fruits of the unchangeable election unto glory, but are conditions, which, being required beforehand, were foreseen as being met by those who will be fully elected, and are causes without which the unchangeable election to glory does not occur."

Finally, we refer to the statement of the Baptism Form:

"And although our young children do not understand these things, we may not therefore exclude them from baptism, for as they are without their knowledge, partakers of the condemnation in Adam, so are they again received unto grace in Christ . . ."

That here none other than the elect children of the covenant are meant and that they are unconditionally, without their knowledge, received unto grace in Christ, in the same way as they are under the condemnation of Adam, is very evident.

C. That faith is not a prerequisite or condition unto salvation, but a gift of God, and a God-given instrument whereby we appropriate the salvation in Christ. This is plainly taught in the following parts of our confessions:

Heidelberg Catechism, {VII} Qu. 20:
{Q. 20.} "Are all men then, as they perished in Adam, saved by Christ?
No; only those who are ingrafted into him, and receive all his benefits, by a true faith."

Netherlands Confession, Art. 22:

{Art. XXII.} "We believe that, to attain the true knowledge of this great mystery, the Holy Ghost kindleth in our hearts an upright faith, which embraces Jesus Christ, with all his merits, appropriates him, and seeks nothing more besides him. For it must needs follow, either that all things, which are requisite to our salvation, are not in Jesus Christ, or if all things are in him, that then those who posses Jesus Christ through faith, have complete salvation in him. Therefore, for any to assert, that Christ is not sufficient, but that something more is required besides him, would be too gross a blasphemy; for hence it would follow, that Christ was but half a Savior. Therefore we justly say with Paul, that we are justified by faith alone, or by faith without works. However, to speak more clearly, we do not mean, that faith itself justifies us, for it is only an instrument with which we embrace Christ our Righteousness. But Jesus Christ, imputing to us all his merits, and so many holy works which he has done for us, and in our stead, is our Righteousness. And faith is an instrument that keeps us in communion with him in all his benefits, which, when become ours, are more than sufficient to acquit us of our sins."

Confer also Netherlands Confession, Articles 33 - 35, quoted above.

Again confer Canons of Dordrecht II, A, 8, quoted above.

In Canons III and IV, A, 10, 14 we read:

{Art. 10.} "But that others who are called by the gospel, obey the call, and are converted, is not to be ascribed to the proper exercise of free will, whereby one distinguishes himself above others, equally furnished with grace sufficient for faith and conversions, as the proud heresy of Pelagius maintains; but it must be wholly ascribed to God, who as he has chosen his own from eternity in Christ, so he confers upon them faith and repentance, rescues them from the power of darkness, and translates them into the kingdom of his own Son, that they may show forth the praises of him, who hath called them out of the darkness into his marvellous light; and may glory not in themselves, but in the Lord according to the testimony of the apostles in various places.

Again in the same chapter of the Canons, Article 14, we read:

{Art. 14.} "Faith is therefore to be considered as the gift of God, not on account of its being offered by God to man, to be accepted or rejected at his pleasure; but because it is in reality conferred, breathed, and infused into him; or even because God bestows the power or ability to believe, and then expects that man should by the exercise of his own free will, consent to the terms of salvation, and actually believe in Christ. But because he who works in man both to will and to do, and indeed all things in all, produces both the will to believe, and the act of believing also."

III. Seeing then that this is the clear teaching of our confession,

    A. We repudiate:

      1. The teaching:

        a. That the promise of the covenant is conditional and for all that are baptized.

        b. That we may presuppose that all the children that are baptized are regenerated, for we know on the basis of Scripture, as well as in the light of all history and experience, that the contrary is true.

{For proof we refer to Canons I, A, 6-8; and the doctrinal part of the Baptismal Form [the latter is quoted];

The Thanksgiving after baptism [is also quoted]

The prayer refers only to the elect; we cannot presuppose that it is for all.}

2. The teaching that the promise of the covenant is an objective bequest on the part of God giving to every baptized child the right to Christ and all the blessings of salvation.

B. And we maintain:
1. That God surely and infallibly fulfills His promise to the elect.
2. That when He so fulfills His promise and establishes His covenant, the elect are not mere stocks and blocks, but obliged and willing to fulfill their part of the covenant, to love their God with all their heart and mind and soul and strength, to forsake the world, to crucify their old nature, and to walk in a new and holy life.
{2.The sure promise of God which He realizes in us as rational and moral creatures not only makes it impossible that we should not bring forth fruits of thankfulness but also confronts us with the obligation of love to walk in a new and holy life, and constantly to watch unto prayer.

All those who are not thus disposed, who do not repent but walk in sin, are the objects of His just wrath and excluded from the kingdom of heaven.

That the preaching comes to all; and that God seriously commands to faith and repentance, and that to all those who come and believe He promises life and peace. Grounds:

a. The Baptism Form, part 3.
b. The Form for the Lord's Supper, under "thirdly": [is quoted]
c. The Heidelberg Catechism XXIV, 64; XXXI, 84; XLV, 116: [all are quoted]
Canons III and IV, A, 12, 16, 17 [all are quoted]
Canons III and IV, B, 9: [is quoted]
Canons V, A, 14: [is quoted]
Netherlands Confession, Article XXIV: [is quoted]}

3. That the ground of infant baptism is the command of God and the fact that according to Scripture He establishes His covenant in the line of continued generations.

IV. Besides, the Protestant Reformed Churches:
A. Cannot condone the action of the Reformed Churches of [should read: *in*] the Netherlands whereby:
1. They imposed certain doctrinal decisions upon the churches synodically, making these decisions binding upon the churches before they had the right to protest.
2. And whereby they deposed many local officebearers.

B. And they believe and maintain the autonomy of the local church.

{IV. Besides, the Protestant Reformed Churches:
Believe and maintain the autonomy of the local church.

For proof we refer to the Netherlands Confession, Article XXXI: [is quoted]

Church Order, Article 36 [is quoted = Canadian Reformed Church Order: Article 37]:

Only the consistory has authority over the local congregation. Church Order, Article 84. [is quoted = Canadian Reformed Church Order: Article 74]

The Form for the Installation of Elders and Deacons:
". . . called of God's Church, and consequently of God himself. . . ."}

*   *   *

If synod adopts the above propositions, we advise:

1. That synod subject this entire document to the approval of the churches.
2. If no objection is offered, to adopt this at our next synod.
3. To adopt this in the meantime as a working hypothesis for our mission committee and for our missionaries in the organization of churches.

Respectfully submitted,

Your committee:

Rev. R. Veltman.
Rev. Gerrit Vos.

Elders: J. Docter
Wm. Huisken.

Advisers: Prof. H. Hoeksema.
Prof. G. M. Ophoff.

[The entire 1950 edition of the Declaration can be found in Article 116 of the Acts of Synod — 1950 of the Protestant Reformed Churches. Article 117 reads:

"Motion is made to accept the document as drawn up by the committee and to act according to the three propositions found at the conclusion of the document. This motion carries.

"Rev. H. Hoeksema volunteers to translate this document into the Holland language."]

Chapter 2
Clear Doctrine?

When we mentioned the text of the *Brief Declaration* we forthwith expressed our opinion that our members who emigrated to America or Canada cannot and may not bind themselves to the *Brief Declaration*. This declaration is being proposed to the local churches of the Protestant Reformed Churches for closer consideration, with the intention of deciding next year whether it can be definitively accepted as a supplementary form of unity, that is, as a more detailed explanation of the existing forms of unity. Because this document, in our opinion, is not clear, our members cannot and may not bind themselves to it. We are also of the opinion that a consistory who would declare this declaration to be binding, and thus would impose it on preaching and education, would create a split between itself and many solidly Reformed people who, on the ground of what Scripture and the confessions tell them, would like to refute this declaration. What do we mean when we speak of refuting? Well, one can refute a (proposed or accepted) binding-formula on two possible grounds. The first ground may be that the declaration is essentially untrue. No one may bind himself or someone else to what is untrue. The second ground may be that the declaration is unclear, confusing, and its formulation ill-defined. Also to such a pronouncement no one can bind himself or someone else without erring in such action. Whatever a church imposes as binding has to be clear, especially when it carries the pretence of clarifying more precisely the existing forms. When such a declaration is not clear then it does not interpret. To interpret means to tell in different (and then clearer) words what is said in the pronouncement that was to be interpreted. Such an explanation has the intention of preventing misunderstanding. However, if something is not clear although it claims to be an explanation, then the misunderstanding increases and the misfortunes are worse than they originally were in connection with the part to be clarified.

*   *   *

For as long as possible we want to keep the newly developed ties from being needlessly severed. Therefore we are very careful. Wherever possible we want to avoid saying, "This is wrong." But we do say: "This is likely to be misunderstood and can already for that reason not be accepted as a binding formula and has to be resisted by every watchdog. These watchdogs would be prevented from 'barking' in freedom (image of Isaiah) if they would be tied up with the chain of such a declaration." An ill-service is rendered to oneself and to others when an unclear statement that creates (or at least allows for) misunderstanding is made into an authoritative statement that has to be accepted in the church as an explanation of the Word of God. An interpreter must speak clearly, especially when he appears as an arbitrator in a doctrinal dispute.

With this viewpoint in mind we would like to have a closer look at that one statement from this American document which states:

"Seeing then that this is the clear *teaching* of our confession, we repudiate the *teaching* that the promise of the covenant is *conditional* and for *all* that are baptized."

This statement evidently alleges that the matter is clear, since it says, "the *clear* teaching of our confession."

Well then, I declare:

a. that speaking about a *teaching* of a conditional promise is only clear as *teaching* when one precisely states what is meant by it. I can be in favour of a certain teaching of conditionality and vehemently opposed to another (for instance the Arminian).

b. that a precise definition is entirely lacking in this American declaration.

c. that therefore the declaration retreats from clearness (of the confession) to confusion (of the new formula).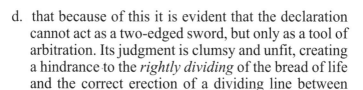

d. that because of this it is evident that the declaration cannot act as a two-edged sword, but only as a tool of arbitration. Its judgment is clumsy and unfit, creating a hindrance to the *rightly dividing* of the bread of life and the correct erection of a dividing line between Reformed and unreformed.

And why? Can one do no better?
Especially theologian Hoeksema is able to distinguish very clearly.

Chapter 3
Rightly Dividing

Rightly dividing. We used this word a little earlier. Everybody knows this expression from Scripture: 2 Timothy 2:15. According to Beza (N.T.) and many others (some write at length about it), this image of rightly dividing (the Word of God) should not make one think of a mother of a family who is slicing a loaf of bread for the members of the family at the table. Bread is of one and the same substance and of equal components in whatever part you put the knife. A clumsy slicer may prepare a thick slice for the one and a thin slice for the other, but every guest receives real bread; the substance is the same for everybody. Although the one may get somewhat less than the other, every participant receives edible food of the same nutritional value. This kind of dividing is not that difficult. But according to the authors mentioned — among whom there are many older Reformed ones — in connection with the word *rightly dividing* one must think of someone who is cutting up an animal for sacrifice, perhaps a hare, or a rabbit, a pheasant, a chicken, or a turkey. However, the one with the knife handles it in all kinds of directions. He must ensure that the result is not that one of the guests receives the nice white meat while an other not more than a few bones. The one should not receive a tough front piece, while the other gets a tender, juicy, T-bone steak.

It does not interest me, for our purpose, whether the opinion concerning 2 Timothy 2:15 is the correct one. There are many more possibilities as far as the exegesis of this text is concerned. But what I want to show is that, even if the writer of 2 Timothy 2:15 did not have this image in mind, this still can be a good reminder for anyone who, in whatever manner, *administers* the Word of God, puts it on the table, and dishes it out to others, especially when believers have to place themselves around the table of unity according to the commandment given to them. Especially then, one has to take care that the *cut* is from the one part as well as from the other part. One must not cling to technical theological terms which have to cover a certain special theological *opinion*.

Then — to use another metaphor — one has to give "the salt with the egg" and "butter with the fish."

In my opinion this does not happen in the above mentioned declaration. The first question to be asked is: "What do you mean with *conditional*?"

Chapter 4
The Voice of the Fathers of Dort

In their opposition to the term *conditional* the writers of the declaration wish to *cut off Arminianism.*

All right. We are strongly in favour of that, inside and outside of the church. But do we really think that our fathers, right after they had *driven out* the Arminians, were naive children, when, for instance they printed the following sentences in a preface to the New Testament in the *Staten Bijbel*:[4]

> "By this (that is, by the word *berith*[5]) the covenant itself is to be understood, which God made with men to give them, under certain *conditions*, eternal life. . . The old covenant is the one God made with the first man before the fall, in which eternal life was promised with the *condition* of a complete obedience and keeping of the law . . . and is therefore called the covenant of the law. God again presented it to the Israelites, in order that they would learn to understand that they had to seek their salvation in another covenant which is called the new covenant and consists of this, that God has ordained His Son to be a Mediator, and promises eternal life under the *condition* that we believe in Him. It is called the *covenant of grace.* These two covenants are one as far as their essence is concerned, because in both of them the forgiveness of sins, salvation, and eternal life are promised under *condition* of believing in the Mediator. But they are distinguished as far as the administration of both is concerned, which in the new covenant is much clearer. . ."

---

[4] Dutch translation of the Bible, by order of the States General of the United Netherlands, in accordance with a decree of the Synod of Dort 1618-19. — Ed.

[5] The word *testament* is a Latin word, meaning Covenant which is *Berith* in Hebrew. — Ed.

The phrase "much clearer" does not mean that in the Old Testament there were *conditions* while in the New there are *no conditions*. Instead, as is clearly indicated, the phrase "much clearer" means that in the Old Testament we find many *types* (figures, shadows, etc.) while in the New Testament we find the *full* reality without the *types*. The *condition remains*, and *also* this becomes much clearer. Yes, this too.

Thus the question remains inescapable: What does one mean with a specific term?

Chapter 5
Be Careful with Dictionaries

We remember that the late Prof. L. Lindeboom once wrote, "be careful with dictionaries." We think of this warning when we listen to the discussions concerning the term *conditions* as a theological and confessional term. Therefore we repeat the question: What does one mean with *conditional*? It would be proof of selfwilled poverty if one, in order to come to clarity on this point, would start perusing in dictionaries of this or that literary expert. One would do better by studying the theological treasures of the fathers who wrote the confessions. There one finds repeated mentioning of *conditions*. The question then is: How does one understand it?

Conditions can mean: rule, position, situation, ordination, or arrangement. It can also have several other meanings.

We will not repeat here what we have already written in brochures, articles, and books. Our opinion can be found in our writings, which as far as we know have been refuted by no one. As far as this concept of the American resolution is concerned, let the following be sufficient:

a. By *condition* do you mean something which would *bind* GOD? Then we say unconditionally: "unconditional is the password!"

b. By *condition* do you mean something *for which* God has to *wait* before He can go on? Then we say unconditionally: "unconditional is the password."

c. By *condition* do you mean something *we* have to fulfil, in order to *merit* something? Then we say unconditionally: "unconditional is the password!"

d. Do you mean by *condition* something which God has *joined to something else*, to make clear to us that the *one* cannot come *without the other* and that we cannot be *sure* of the one, unless we are at the same time *assured* of the other? Then we say unconditionally: "conditional is the password!"

Chapter 6
Bad *Condition* Theories

What is said above needs some explanation.

a. God is *not* bound by anything but only by His *Own* determined will, His *Own* fixed decree or counsel, and His *Own* good pleasure which He fulfils in His *Own* way and time. In His sovereign good pleasure He has decreed that only the elect will effectively obtain the benefits which He has promised in the covenant of grace to those who believe in Him. He has elected certain people to salvation and *thus* to faith, hope, love, and all that can and has to follow. Election is election; it is free, unchangeable, and particular. God has chosen the elect to be drawn out of total death and therefore He cannot make *conditions* which had to *move* Him to elect them or would authorize Him to do it. He chooses on the ground of His good pleasure and for no other reason. Whatever the elect *yield* of faith, hope, or love, in short, of good works, they can only *yield* out of the power that He Himself has granted to them in free grace, according to His eternal good pleasure.

b. Therefore, God doesn't have to *wait* for anything. He doesn't have to wait for one who is dead to come. For a dead person does not come, unless he comes from death to life. And this making-alive lies only with God the Lord Himself, Who is the One who makes alive by His own unique (*proprium*) work.[6] He doesn't have to *wait* for anything before He elects. He doesn't have to wait for anything before He, for instance, takes *to Himself,* little children who die in their infancy, because He takes care of His Own work as is intended in the case of the children mentioned in the Canons of Dort I, 17. He doesn't have to *wait* for anything with adults, whom He has called by His Word, for when He, in their life, wants to say A, then He says A. When God wants to say B, then He does it, yet always considering the sequence which He Himself made for His Own work, where the B follows the A. That is in all cases in which He has decided that an A should be written before a B. And if it pleases Him to write a B, a C, a D, or a Z, in a different way, then He does it, wherever He wills. We think of insane people for instance, who are not able to believe or confess in an ordinary way and whom He, as far as it pleases Him, will bring to salvation.

c. Since it all happens *freely*, *merit* is completely out of the picture. It wasn't there in Paradise and after that even less. It is actually foolish in this connection to think in terms of *more* or *less*; earning anything is principally excluded, also with Adam, the inhabitant of Paradise, who was righteous before God. Faith is therefore no *merit* and faith is never a *ground* for salvation and neither is repentance.

---

[6] To prevent misunderstanding; this we say under reservation of what we have noted about this *Own work* of God in my book: *Heidelbergsche Catechismus*, vol. III (Goes: Oosterbaan & Le Cointre, 1951) (see index).

Chapter 7
Good *Condition* Theory

d. Now we come to the fine point: God gives us *promises* but no predictions. So, He does not say to one person, "One day, you will be in heaven," and to another, "You will eternally remain outside of it." He gives a *promise with a command*, as it says in the Canons of Dort: "the *promise* comes with the *command* to *repent* and *believe*" (Canons of Dort, II, 5). Therefore He says at baptism: "Whosoever believeth on Him shall not be ashamed" (Romans 10:11); "for them that honour Me I will honour" (1 Samuel 2:30); "Unto the upright there ariseth light in the darkness" (Psalm 112:4); "those that seek Me early shall find Me" (Proverbs 8:17).

And whoever wants to call this view Arminian does not read his Bible properly, by which indeed the Arminians were defeated.

In conclusion we ask, "Why would one use terms which cannot profit anybody?" The whole passage about *unconditional* is introduced (see the beginning of C) with the remark:

a. faith is not a *prerequisite.*
b. faith is not a *condition* for salvation, not a required condition.

But we all agree with that! At least when we understand it properly. The declaration says: *faith is not a prerequisite unto salvation, BUT a gift of God.* Any meaning put in the word *condition,* causing it to mean that faith is not *given* but *comes* from ourselves, will be rejected wholeheartedly by all of us! How can one think differently? Why would we then accept the term *prerequisite* as if faith were a requirement of which the fulfilment would precede the *counsel* of God?

All of this is Arminian foolishness, which we in the Netherlands do not want anything to do with.

But, as a result of this confusing interpretation we ask, "Why don't you speak clearly?" You say that faith is not a *prerequisite*? We agree if by *prerequisite* you mean the same as when I say that the work of the hired man must precede his wages.

Again, we agree if the meaning of *prerequisite* is the same as when I say that the girl must have pleased the young man before he asked her to marry him. Faith does not precede God's decree for our salvation, nor God's calling. Of course not. But faith does precede the *attaining* of our full salvation. For faith even precedes our *regeneration*, according to Article 24 of the *Belgic Confession*. The A does not come before the B in God's decree to design an alphabet. But it does in the life of them whom the Lord according to the ordinary rule will lead to salvation.

I think colleague Hoeksema will agree with us in all of this. That is also why we *appeal* to him. He is a sharp theologian and he hates all foolish binding. Let him cooperate to prevent unclear and unpractical statements, which are one of the many impediments on the road to church-unity. Let him not force our people to start yet an other church, where his own churches are called to gather the people of God in that vast America. *Much* can still be *prevented* so that the light of the truth will remain clear and bright. Unclear declarations obstruct this clear shining. Colleague Hoeksema certainly does not want this. We must only stick to terms if they are gateways through which the truth accordingly can enter.

Chapter 8
Summary

We summarize what has been said until now as follows:
The above mentioned American declaration is not clear, for one can reject conditional promises, and still emphasize that it all depends on how you interpret the word *conditional*.

A church which wants to bind men by an *unclear* formula, even if it is only temporarily as a *working hypothesis*, does not act according to the command of God for the gathering of His church. The church has to be clear in her binding. What counts is not that it obediently confesses an unclear term, but that it adheres to the *clear doctrine* of the Scriptures with heart and soul and *confesses* it with the mouth. Let those in America please show the Arminians the door. We do it too. But never give in, not even one step, to the foolishness — which will soon turn to judgment — with which the whole affair was spoiled in the Netherlands in 1944. At that time a non-existent Arminianism was imagined in certain quarters, while the real Arminians were left alone in aspirations for the world-council-of-churches associations and in professorial speeches of the Free University, about which also Prof. Van der Schuit appeared to be concerned. Don't ever let this happen in America. Do not become guilty of abandoning Reformed people because they speak of conditional promises, as long as they do that precisely in the manner of the church fathers, who had just driven out the Arminians.

Chapter 9
A New Point

This is how it stands with the pronouncement that the promises are only *for the elect.* We read in the concept of the Protestant Reformed Churches some expressions which are worth the effort to contemplate.

Chapter 10
Cause or *Ground?*

First a small remark. The declaration (II, A) starts with the expression: "that election . . . is the *sole cause* and *fountain* of all our salvation." Is this properly expressed in a binding statement? Of course, we ourselves may have said the same thing, perhaps sometimes in a loose article or a speech or so. We will not blame anybody who expresses himself in less than duly considered terminology. But if one is going to *fix* and *bind*, then we say: "Wait a minute!" When the declaration states that *election* is the *cause* and *fountain* is it using theoretically precise, accurate, scholarly terminology? *good*

I don't believe it! To be accurate it should say: "Election is the *ground*." A decree of God is never the *cause* of its execution, nor its *fountain*. Cause and fountain happen in time and are themselves also included in the *decree*. In order to draw closer together, I quote a strongly supralapsarian theologian. I am not supralapsarian, but neither am I infralapsarian, because I believe with Bavinck that the dilemma as such is not allowed in our speaking about God. But, if I have understood it properly, more than one theologian on "the other side" have sympathized with Kuyper, and thus with supralapsarianism. However, we do acknowledge, also here, the elements of truth which are found in this supralapsarian system of thought. That is why I choose a supralapsarian: Twissus.

Twissus (*In Arn. Corvini Defensionem Sententiae Jac. Arminii De Praedestinatione, Gratia et Lib. Arbitrio, & c., Amstelodami, 1649, 257, a*) speaks about the question whether the will of God is *conditional*, yes or no.

Some people are assured that the will of God as *will* is absolute, not *conditional*.

"Now," says Twissus, "they may be right in saying this. In this way the matter is somewhat more accurately expressed. But," says our supralapsarian, "don't be too hasty and take care not to run too far away with it. For you can also say with good intention that the will of God is *conditional*. You can also be properly Reformed in saying: There are *two kinds* of God's will, one which is absolute and one which is *conditional*. You can speak of God's will as conditional if you are not strictly looking at God's *actions* as God wills them — for looking at God's actions as He wills them, God's will is always absolute — but rather you wish to speak about the *things* which are willed by God in

modal
→ *fallacy*

these *actions*. For God Himself wills that certain things *absolutely* happen and that other things only happen under certain *conditions* (in relation to certain circumstances, see above).

"In that sense God *absolutely* wills faith, regeneration, and repentance for His elect. This means that He *absolutely* wills that these gifts *be performed in them*. And, indeed, that they will come. Now the same God — take note, we are still talking about the elect! — has bound their salvation to faith and repentance and the ultimate perseverance. He wants this salvation, thus, on condition of faith, repentance, and perseverance."

Do not now accuse Twissus of being a heretic! Do not push Twissus outside the church with a brief declaration. It would be a pity for Twissus and for your church.

The supralapsarian Twissus wouldn't for a second think of asserting that faith, repentance, and perseverance are *meriting* causes of salvation. Twissus doesn't for a single second get it in his brain to teach that God has to wait passively and *depends* on that faith, that repentance, and that perseverance, and that otherwise He cannot give His salvation-benefits to you.

Twissus would direct his gaze on us with a bemused smile. On his face we would read the question, "How in the world can you think so foolishly and blame me for such foolish Arminian heresy." He would say, "Please stop; I certainly have taught you better than that!" But he would add to it, "Don't run away like a horse, but rather reconsider and study the matter. God, from His side, has ordained that the evening follows the afternoon and noon follows the morning. So, if He promises me that in my evening I will see the salvation of the Lord, then it is self evident that I first have to go through morning and afternoon. This is definitely not something earned, nor is it a *condition* which makes Him dependent."

If a supralapsarian can speak in this way, can't the American brothers learn what Twissus taught? The salvation of the elect is *absolutely* willed by God, but under *condition* of faith, repentance, and perseverance, and therefore He *absolutely will take care* that we receive these benefits from Him.

Where will we end up, if we abandon our best people with formulas without considering the question involved?

Chapter 11
"Cause," a Term Easily Misunderstood

Well then, in connection with these simple matters, it will have its meaning when we say: be careful now, do not confuse *ground* and *cause*. When I declare — and with the pretention of the greatest accuracy in a new binding — that election is the *cause* and *fountain* of our total salvation, then I run the danger of making someone, and later the whole church, think that if election is present then the *fountain* is bubbling, the *cause* is working, and the process is on its way. "No," says Twissus, "nothing is going on yet." He admonished the Arminians, especially Corvinus, three times (page 263, a) not to confuse election with the *execution of election*. Decree and the realization of the decree are two different matters. Election is not the cause. With election, the decree is from eternity. When I merely *decide* to travel to Amsterdam, then nothing as yet has *happened*.

The cause of my coming to Amsterdam is that I finally did put on my coat, went to the railway station and said goodbye to the silhouette of my residence.

When I decide to do something then *this* decision can still change for at first I did not make a decision at all, or perhaps I would have decided something different, for instance to travel to London. But in God all decisions are unchangeable, a decision or decree therefore does not change anything in Him. Nor in us. That which causes anything in us and which is thus *cause* and *fountain* of *all salvation*, is something which comes in time. The *causes* all work with and in time. Of course the brothers in America know that as well as we do. However, we continue.

"Well then," Twissus says to Corvinus, "you better quit accusing us of wrong reasoning in the manner of, for instance, making up a chain reasoning as follows:

a. the Reformed assert that election is the cause and fountain of all salvation.

b. a fountain, which God makes to flow, will give water. A cause which God puts to work will work.

c. thus the Reformed teach that the elect will surely believe; he cannot do otherwise. Who can stop a fountain which God set flowing?

d. consequently, the Reformed make people heedless, lazy, and careless. Fine pastors they are, those Reformed teachers!

"Man, stop," Twissus now says, "you are forgetting that the decree, strictly speaking, is not the fountain or the cause. We do not tell our children and our people, 'you are elect, for that is what your baptism indicates and you may now conclude that the stream of God's clear healing water has started to flow.' No," says Twissus, "you Arminians forget one thing. The doctrine of election is not a doctrine of causes or fountains. Causes and fountains only occur in history, in what God started in this world. For instance, and that certainly in the first place, the *preaching of the Word* is a cause and a fountain. That is where the fountain starts to spout water. There the cause is working.

"There is a *causa efficax*, that means, a cause that has working-power (an effective cause), although you should not say," Twissus adds, "that it is now already really efficient, already concretely reaching the goal" (*In Arminii cum Iunio de Praed. Coll. Animadc.*, 25, a).

Consequently, we do not make people rely upon election, as ground and fountain, but upon *the Word.*

I agree with that.

Chapter 12
Beginning of the Work of Grace in Us

"And as it hath pleased God, *by* the preaching of the gospel (there is the cause and fountain, K.S.), to begin this work of grace in us, so He preserves, continues, and perfects it by the hearing and reading of His Word, by meditation thereon, and by the exhortations, threatenings, and promises thereof, as well as by the use of the sacraments" (Canons of Dort V, 14).

When I come across these words in the Canons of Dort I would like to say in connection with this: If I go to America and attempt to join the church known to be based on the Three Forms of Unity and on nothing besides them until a short while ago, and they would say: "Come in, but first sign this declaration," I would reply, "I am disappointed; I thought that you had learned from Kalamazoo;[7] *I will not sign it now.*" I would have been pleased to listen if it had not been a formula that had to serve as a criterion. But since it *is*, I will not sign it, and the fault is not with me, when our ways part until better times. I presented myself and I consider myself to be Reformed, and I do not go out of the way in this respect for anyone who also calls himself Reformed. Are they supralapsarian? So was Twissus. Yet Twissus said that election is not the fountain, nor the cause, but the *ground.* The cause is *the Word,* including its *threats.*

A threat is senseless if you let the gospel consist only of an ill-defined, unconditional promise. *Unconditional* is a term with a thousand possible meanings. Twissus said that even the salvation of the elect God wills conditionally, under a condition which He Himself will create. However, He binds me to His Word with threats, for *predicting* is different than *promising.*

---

[7] It was at the Synod held at Kalamazoo that Rev. Hoeksema was expelled from the Christian Reformed Church since he refused to let himself be bound by an unholy binding to poorly considered declarations, as we see it, concerning (alleged) "common grace."

Chapter 13
Theorems

Now we come to the afore mentioned expressions which we have to consider a little closer.

Here they are:

a. "that all the covenant blessings are for the elect alone." (Take note: it says *blessings*. Is the calling also a blessing, and therefore also only for the elect?)

b. "that the promise of the gospel . . . concerns only the believers, that is, the elect." (Question: what does this difficult term, *concern*, mean, about which many philosophers are writing?)

c. "if the *promise* of God *is* for them (the little children), than the promise has to be *infallible* and *unconditional* and can *therefore only concern the elect*." (Question: what is now meant by this new term, infallible? Is Calvin no longer allowed to say that someone, by unbelief, can make God's promise *irrita*, — that is, not realized — because the promise, by avoiding the form of prediction, was only given in the manner of Twissus as a promise of the *evening* blessing — eternal salvation — under the condition of *listening to the Word* in the *morning* and at *noon*?)

d. *"Hence, that promise is surely only for the elect."*

Chapter 14
Infallible Concern

There we are again.

Infallible. Again a word which one in a well defined sense must maintain unconditionally, but which one in a different sense may quietly consider as irrelevant. The question may be asked whether salvation can bypass someone who is baptized with a promise with its attached demand and threat, *without* God having lied or having let the church lie, or . . . utter empty talk. If indeed God has threatened something like that beforehand to unbelievers then His *CONCRETE* proclamation becomes *infallibly* true.

There we stand again.

What does *concern* mean? Is it a legal claim? If so then we say the promise concerns EVERYONE to whom it comes. Infallibly. Or . . . does it mean progress from being *effiCAX* to being *effiENT* for the goal of God's purpose: the salvation of the elect? *Then we say: unconditionally ONLY* for the elect.

Here we stand once again.

What is the meaning of *are for* in the sentence *the covenant blessings are for the elect alone*? Does it mean lawfully and legally affecting the addressed man to the letter, seizing him and putting him for all eternity under an unremovable claim? Then we say "*It is for everybody.*" Or does *are for* mean: to have in your hands the final fibres of the promised garment of salvation, defined by Twissus' condition, and to receive that shining apparel around your glorified body? Then we say, "Please say it clearly: '*only for the elect.*'"

There we stand. A formula that can go in all directions, and still be made binding? Does such a formula bring anyone further? In our opinion, it does not.

Chapter 15
Dogmatic Statement or Address?

The big question that now appears is: What *happens* at baptism? Do I receive a dogmatic statement: God brings all the elect to salvation? Or am I addressed with a *legal statement*, in which I am personally and individually involved?

Examples of dogmatic statements are: "God created the world," or "Christ's blood justifies," or "Mary did not ascend bodily into heaven," or "If the weather is beautiful, then God has done this."

However, to receive a dogmatic statement is not sufficient for me. I don't want a statement but an *address*. Therefore the big question is: *what* do we receive at our *baptism*?

There we are. How can we sail the Pacific (I quote Twissus, somewhat mischievously)? No, of course, you don't read that in Twissus. He tells the Arminians (in Corv. 257a) that they with their doctrine of a foreseen faith as ground for election, can as easily philosophize as they can organize a sailing trip on a calm sea, a *mare pacificum*. A pacific sea is of course not the Pacific Ocean. Still, we have to cross all the oceans of time . . . till later; until the horizon is reached and we arrive at that gate on which God has written: *salus* (which Twissus called the terminus; *salus* means eternal salvation at the end of the track). Whatever our course of life is, the Pacific or the Atlantic Ocean, the all decisive question remains how did I get on that ship? Was I put there with a beautiful, philosophical, dogmatic, orthodox *statement* that salvation is only for the elect, because: a) . . ., b) . . ., c) . . ., d) . . ., and so on? Or am I placed on this ship with a *promise*, an *admonition*, a *threat*, a *stipulation* here, and a *stipulation* there? How do I sail?

This is the matter in question and because of that we like to make a few remarks about the words "are for."

Chapter 16
Are For

What is the implication of the statement: "the promise is for all" (who are lawfully baptized in a church of Christ). We have already shown why we deemed it more than necessary that before exposing the church to calamities by completely unnecessary controversies, people should say precisely what is to be understood by the words: "are for" (the promise *is for* all, or *it is only for the elect*).

If the words "are for" mean that the promise creates a *legal* connection and acknowledges the already existing connection and also puts the baptized person individually under *legal* claims, then we say the promise is for all.

If, however, someone wants the expression "are for" to be understood in the sense that one will receive, for all eternity the promised contents, down to the last cent, then we assure you that the promise is only for the elect.

It must be clear by now that one does not get very far with a formula unless a clear distinction is made.

Chapter 17
Common Grace

We received a copy of the *Standard Bearer* in which colleague Hoeksema gives a more detailed explanation of the proposed declaration.

In it he writes something about *common grace*.

Our readers know and appreciate how Hoeksema, who has done courageous and necessary work in the case of the *common grace* theory, will guard the churches he is serving so as to prevent that dangerous doctrine, which he condemned and rejected, from creeping in again. Since it is good that we don't argue alongside of each other, it is even more important that the misunderstandings, by which the devil would like to choke all flourishing church-work, may be cleared up as much as possible in a business like fashion. For that reason we are going to deal with this new objection.

Let us try to understand the American brothers.

*   *   *

I read in the above mentioned issue of the *Standard Bearer* (Oct. 1, 1950 — vol. 27, no. 1, p. 6 and 7) that the proposed American declaration will be as accurate concerning the theory of *common grace*, as it is concerning the promise of the covenant. Of course, we are happy with that. We have also seen the *common grace* theorem going limp on both legs; we therefore resisted it and we believe that that struggle bore fruit. When a synod began hacking with a Chinese scimitar, we were compelled to express ourselves in an exact formulation about the promise of the covenant of grace, over against a petrified groups-theology which did not know the Reformed fathers — evidenced by the enormous mistakes made by Dr. A. D. R. Polman in 1944. In this way we were able to open the way to Helenius De Cock, which the Kuyperian diehards had blocked, and to break open again the path to the classic fathers, whose books had been made inaccessible. We believe that also on this point the work has been blessed.

We do not say this to boast against that synod of 1944. We only mention it because we would love to see this little straw fire, which is threatening to flare up between America and us, stamped out from both sides. Here in the Netherlands we have to understand well that in 1924 the American men were faced with the same matters as we were in 1944 and that neither they nor we started our own *affairs* for our own enjoyment. If we begin to understand this, and appreciate this from one another, then my intention with these articles, namely to prevent our emigrants from being forced to *start a separate affair*, can be better understood. Starting separate affairs is what sectarians do, also those who take an existing broad basis (Three Forms of Unity) and make it much narrower; those who of a universal matter make a particular affair, as did the synodocracy,[8] with all its denying-*power* which she still will not be able to deny with *authority* (*exousia*).

I would like to make one more remark which may help to bring peace. Colleague Hoeksema says emphatically that the proposed declaration of principles "cannot possibly be directed against the *Liberated Churches*." He acknowledges — I am pleased with that and please let it remain that way in the *Standard Bearer* — "that they claim that as churches they have not accepted any official covenant conception." That is completely correct as long as he means a different conception than the one which is found in the confession.

---

[8] The author is referring to the synodical dealings in the Netherlands from 1942-1944. — Ed.

Those we have indeed accepted. "At most, therefore," says
colleague Hoeksema, "it should be said that it [the
declaration, Ed.] is directed at some of the Liberated, who
assert that the promise of God is objectively for all the
baptized children and that in this promise God is gracious to
them all."

I don't know whom colleague Hoeksema has in mind.
Apparently he is thinking of certain people. I don't know
them, but I do sometimes read very hastily. I will not pursue
the question of whether an ecclesiastical assembly is wise in
drawing up a declaration directed against a few people in a
foreign country. Let us however remain on the safe side and
say, "O.K., bring your weapons of defense into position
against any dangers that threaten, including any which may
come from the side of individual persons." But also then I
want to ask, "what do these men mean, when, in citations
not known to me, they said that God, in His promise, is
gracious to all baptized children. What aroused suspicion,
making a declaration of principles necessary for a defense?"

Chapter 18
Heynsianism

Involuntarily we start searching for what dangers they
perceive. We do find some indications in the article of
colleague Hoeksema. He fears that in one way or another
the concept of Heyns, which he previously had resisted,
would creep in again. Heyns taught a certain common grace
within the circle of the covenant and when one now says
that the promise is for all, don't we again run the risk of
sailing into Heynsian waters?

To this I would like to answer that also when resisting
Heyns, you must be able to point out where he goes wrong.
For a long time I asked myself which Heynsian concept the
Protestant Reformed brothers thought should be opposed.
No more than Kuyper should become a bogey or legend in

the Netherlands, should Heyns become such in America. One should always be able to indicate exactly which point is wrong and must be done away with.

During my latest stay in America I ran into a work by Heyns (two volumes if I remember well), which I have never seen in the Netherlands, in which specific statements were pointed out to me. Then a discerning minister said to me, "Look, there is the problem." And indeed, he pointed out some expressions where Heyns went wrong. Doing so was a good thing, it helped prevent seeing ghosts. I then studied those expressions and wrote against them saying that we don't believe that either. You can read it in *de Reformatie* of Oct. 25, 1947.

Chapter 19
An Old Statement

The first problem with Heyns concerned the matter of the so called *subjective Covenant-grace,* about which I wrote the following:

> "Parallel with it follows a long row of statements by Heyns about *subjective Covenant-grace.* The imparting of a certain measure of subjective grace also belongs, in his opinion, to the benefits of the covenant.[9] It differs from the grace of regeneration. Referring to John 15:2, Romans 11:17, and Isaiah 5:4, this subjective Covenant-grace, which is also for the reprobates in the covenant, is called "a grace which takes from the Covenant member all excuse for not bringing forth the desired fruit of the Covenant."[10]

---

[9] W. Heyns, *Gereformeerde Geloofsleer* (*G.G.*) (2nd Edition, Sneek: J. W. Boeijenga Zonen, 1927), p. 136; translated by the author, W. Heyns, as *Manual of Reformed Doctrine* (Grand Rapids: Wm. B. Eerdmans, 1926), p. 134. — Ed.

[10] Ibid., p. 137

Now we can shake our heads and remark that the objective-subjective scheme plays a trick on the author. This is true. Also in other places he apparently falls victim to this.

However, such a complaint (which would also strike many of his opponents) still does not reach the basic difference. Here in this part of the *G.G.* Heyns does not go farther than to say that this subjective Covenant-grace takes away from the disobedient members of the covenant all excuses for NOT bringing forth the DESIRED fruit of the covenant.

This is rather negative and careful.

Somewhere else, though, he writes positively and carelessly, and most certainly erroneously.

This is especially true in his *Handboek voor de Catechetiek* (unknown in the Netherlands). Americans know the whole of Heyns, while we in the Netherlands only know half of Heyns. This may be the cause of the misunderstandings. How fatal they can be, appeared to me, when Heyns in different places again mentions the texts Isaiah 5:4, John 15:2, and Romans 11:17 (for instance in *Handboek* 143/4). There Heyns definitely goes the wrong way. The topic of the removal of all excuses keeps him busy again, but now he falls into the trap of scolasticism and schematism. When Isaiah 5:4 asks, "What more was there to do at My vineyard, that I have not done in it?" then Heyns writes, "Would He, Who is the true One, ask this? Would He be able to ask this, if what He had done to them had only consisted of outward working without giving the internal susceptibility for it?"[11]

Internal susceptibility!

Is it any wonder that the complaint of Arminianism comes up? Or the complaint that here the total depravity and the radical wickedness and the powerlessness-in-unwillingness is diminished? Or the

---

[11] W. Heyns, *Handboek voor de Catechetiek* (Grand Rapids: Eerdmans-Sevensma Co., 1907), p. 144.

question of the spiritual gifts which can be lost? One cannot blame all this on misunderstanding, for some lines farther we read, "If one wants to do justice to such expressions one has to come to the conclusion, whether one likes it or not, that Scripture teaches us that each member of the covenant receives the gift of subjective grace. Each child of believers receives *sufficient to produce good fruits.* This gift is for all members of the covenant, not only for the elect."[12]

To be honest, I was astonished by this expression. I was not aware of it, nor of the book, and had considered it impossible for him to say this.

So impossible did I find this expression, that, for a moment, I even tried to get out of it by removing from the word *gift* its meaning of *actual granting* in the quote cited above. I realized that in another context, according to this author, *to give* means something else than *making us participants.*[13]

Yet, even with this distinction I still cannot work as an apologist for Heyns. This is because his scholastic question mentioned above, "How would God, in Isaiah 5:4, be able to ask?" proves that by using *to give* with reference to that subjective Covenant-grace, does not mean a promise but a making of partakers in reality.

And that is wrong. None of us *repeats* this after Heyns, we all REJECT it.

We can see here how fatal it is when one link of the chain hooks into the other and in both cases the problem is stated unclearly.

For also here the common-grace-idea with its false Kuyperian epic is running through the author's head. He says, "Concerning the covenant with Noah, we believe that it has been accompanied by the benefaction of a measure of more common grace, with such an increase of common subjective grace (! K.S.) that mankind, by its sin-resistant action, would be saved

---

[12] Ibid.

[13] *Manual*, p. 134; compare p. 269.

from sinking a second time into a deluge of iniquity as before the flood, and would be able to inherit the promise of that covenant. Why would it be unacceptable then, that the so much more glorious covenant with Abraham has been accompanied with the giving of subjective grace to all members of the covenant, with the result that the total *insusceptibility*, of natural men to the things which are of the Spirit of God, is taken away to the extent that the members of the covenant have an *initial susceptibility?*"[14]

What is proposed here is apparently that we receive communal grace, which at least temporarily sets aside the totality of total incapability. Grace which can be lost! We no longer have total depravity of the unregenerate!

Later Heyns manoeuvres around a bit by saying that the catechist has a warranty in the covenant; that "the seed of the covenant has received from God susceptibility for *impressions* by His (God's) covenant labour." But this feeble language is too weak to be a reproduction of what was stated earlier. Heyns says that for all members of the covenant, by virtue of this subjective Covenant-grace, "they [these impressions] are (for the catechist) regarded as NOT unsuitable material."[15]

I am very glad to have read this passage. Finally I understand the total depth and necessity of Hoeksema's struggle and I pity the Christian Reformed Church which has rid itself of this helper. This man who already earlier, when others failed or had to lean on him, had helped them out of the swamp and rightly reacted against this blunting of the Reformed broadsword. What weaklings there are all over the place. First they mess things up and later, terrified that their work will cause a crisis or that people will wake up, give stately decrees to the world not to listen to the

---

[14] *Handboek*, p. 145.

[15] Ibid., p. 146.

ones whom they in their foolishness have thrown out. Why? I think it is good in this connection to repeat that our churches do NOT have a different view of the covenant beside that which we have in the Forms and therefore as churches we reject the rubbish of the Grosheide-committee versus "candidate H. J. Schilder," as well as the formulas to which they bound us. To that we add the contents of Heyns' book, for not one of our theologians, as far as I know, could even imagine agreeing with Heyns in these matters. Not only because we do not draw *such consequences,* but also because from the beginning we have stood squarely opposed to such speculating. If someone brought this Heynsian wisdom to the fore, the churches would reject it on the ground of the existing confession.

Finally, Heyns quotes more than once the text of Jeremiah 8:22: "Is there no balm in Gilead; is there no physician there? Why then is not the health of the daughter of my people recovered?" This text — we will let the translation and the exegesis rest for now — is put beside the above mentioned texts as support for the doctrine of subjective Covenant-grace and its making all (also the not elected) members of the covenant susceptible. Elsewhere[16] this same statement comes to the fore to make the thesis of the *well meant* offer of salvation more acceptable.

Now among us there is not one who would want to object to the Canons of Dort when they declare that God, through the gospel calls *earnestly,* "earnestly and most sincerely." However, there is also not one among us, I think, who does not realize that, after all the hocus pocus we talked about earlier, the phrase *well meant* received a meaning which differs from the words (earnestly and most sincerely) of the Canons and that along with it the term *offer* here received an unreformed flavour, different from that of the Canons of Dort (*oblatus* and *offerre*). The misinterpretation-complex

---

[16] *Manual,* p. 191

of Heyns culminates in a discussion of the faith. According to Heyns the *assured confidence*, from Lord's Day 7, "which the Holy Spirit works by the Gospel in my heart; that not only to others, but to me also, remission of sin, everlasting righteousness and salvation, are freely given by God, merely of grace," is to be understood in the sense that *freely given* means here *to offer!* He says, "The intention is to describe faith as a firm confidence in the offer of salvation. God has granted means: God has offered."[17]

But trusting in an offer is different than trusting that that which is offered has also been given.

We'll let this go for now, but we do ask, "Is it any wonder that opposition arose against this theory?" No, for a few lines earlier (*G.G.* 264) Heyns remarked that *to give* has the meaning of *to offer* also in those cases "in which the one to whom it is given is also able to appropriate it."

If all this would make sense, then the speaker in Lord's Day 7 would be confessing his faith in his own faith. But he confesses his faith in God and in His PROMISES, knowing that the benefits for him are FIRM and SURE.

Even of the trust itself, he confesses that the Spirit worked it by the gospel. But about that preparatory grace and its effect (of capability) on which one makes progress in building up, he does not say a word.

I hope from the heart that I have given a desired clarification of our position.

So far our citation [from *de Reformatie* of Oct. 25, 1947].

---

[17] *G.G.*, p. 265. In his English translation Heyns wrote, "the expression of Qu. 21: 'an assured confidence that everlasting righteousness and salvation, are freely given by God' must mean: an assured confidence, not that we have been partakers of it by faith, but that it is freely given us by God, or an assured confidence in the Gospel, in the offer of salvation" (*Manual*, p. 269f). Heyns translated freely and changed the context somewhat. — Ed.

Chapter 20
Maintained Statement

Were our words not clear enough? I can't see it.

Did I picture the situation amongst our theologians too favourably? I can't see it. Did we later pass off the matter too hastily? I can't admit it. On the contrary. In my explanation of the Catechism (vol. 2) I have extensively written about the word *Offer*, and also about the word *well meant* (Dutch: ernstig). Unless I am greatly mistaken, it has been forwarded to colleague Hoeksema.

Now the conclusion. I'd like to do everything to remove the misunderstandings. But it is just for that reason that I may and must beg you not to place us in a Heynsian twilight. We meant what we said and I don't know any one among us who objected to what I wrote about Heyns.

Therefore I don't believe that when we say that the promise is for all who are baptized (that is to say the promise places them in a legal status which is tighter and therefore more stringent than that in which the unbaptized find themselves) we thereby introduce common grace theories. No way. The administration of the Word gives a proper savour of Christ, Paul says, if it is administered so that for the one it is a savour of death unto death, and to the other the savour of life unto life. I wish that we may be permitted to think as Paul did and to teach as Paul did and not to say that he who considers the service of the Word as a promise-service only makes it a common-grace-perfume business. Far from it. If I see dangers, and this is actually the case, then the danger is this, that one preaches that the savour *from death to death* is separated from the proper service of the Word. We do not say that with the right hand God spreads a savour of life (and this is His *proper* work *opus proprium*) but with the left hand God spreads a savour of death (and that is His *strange* work *opus alienum*). We leave such nonsense to the young Luther and to the old Barth.[18]

---

[18] See note in Chapter 6 concerning our remarks about God's *Own* or *proper* works (and in connection with this about God's "right- and left hand" work).

Chapter 21
What is *Behind* it?

Above we have clearly rejected the Heynsian construction which we knew had offended — and rightly so — the leaders of the Protestant Reformed Churches. I also remarked that, as far I know, no one among us thought or wrote differently than I myself had already done for years. Therefore, I still ask the question: "What is behind it?" In order to find out as much as possible I will give part of the answer which colleague Hoeksema gave to Rev. Blankespoor, one of the ministers of the Protestant Reformed Churches (from the *Standard Bearer* of Oct. 1, 1950).

Rev. Blankespoor asked colleague Hoeksema a question which started as follows:

> "I am informed that the Mission Committee requested Synod to draw up a form regarding our principles for those (especially in Canada) who request organization. On the basis of this synod drew up this declaration."

Part of colleague Hoeksema's answer is as follows (with mission work is meant: labours among such who think differently):

> "We used to conduct this kind of mission work chiefly in the Christian Reformed Churches. And the work used to concentrate chiefly around the question of common grace as adopted by the Christian Reformed Church in 1924 and embodied in the well-known Three Points. With this work I am personally thoroughly acquainted, as I used to go out for weeks at a time to explain the errors of the Three Points, especially to the Christian Reformed people in Illinois, Wisconsin, Iowa, and even in California. It was never our purpose simply to extend our churches and to

organize congregations. Always the people were first acquainted with our standpoint and our Protestant Reformed truth in distinction from the errors of the Three Points. And it was only after they were convinced of these errors and as a result of these labors a group was gathered that were willing to subscribe to our Protestant Reformed principles, that they were organized into a church.

"Recently, however, the Mission Committee faced what was really the same problem from a different angle. They and our missionaries came into contact with people that are apparently willing to subscribe to our denial of common grace and to repudiate the Three Points, but who insist that the promise is for all the children that are born under the historical dispensation of the covenant. In other words, they wanted to maintain common grace within the historical line of the covenant. These people had their origin in the Reformed Churches of the Netherlands. Historically as well as doctrinally they differed from the Christian Reformed Churches in America, but also from our Protestant Reformed Churches. In the Netherlands they had been urged to join the Protestant Reformed Churches and not the Christian Reformed Church. No wonder then, that they lived under the impression that they could simply, without further instruction, be organized into Protestant Reformed Churches. But at the same time they wanted to adhere to their own peculiar view of the covenant. They even sent a request to the Mission Committee to be organized on their own basis. That was the difficulty with which the Mission Committee had to contend.

"Hence, the Mission Committee wanted a definite form as a basis for the organization of churches, a form on the basis of which our missionaries could labor among these people, and which they themselves could study in order that they might not only become acquainted with our view, but also know what they were doing when they requested the Mission

Committee for organization into Protestant Reformed Churches."

This is followed by an account stating that the declaration has not yet been definitely accepted. Our readers already know this. After this the following question by Rev. Blankespoor is mentioned:

"It seems to me that the declaration is mainly directed at the Liberated Churches. Only a small portion is given to the repudiation of the common grace theory, church hierarchy, etc., while a large portion, directly and indirectly, is devoted to the repudiation of the Liberated views of the covenant and baptism. Am I correct in drawing this conclusion?"

To this colleague Hoeksema answers:

"The declaration of principles cannot possibly be directed against the *Liberated Churches*, for the simple reason that they claim that as churches they have no covenant conception. They claim that in their churches there is nothing binding concerning the covenant.
"Of course, the question is how far this goes. I discussed our difficulties with Mr. and Mrs. A. Schilder, brother and sister-in-law of the professor. They were over last summer and we had the privilege of entertaining them at our home for a couple of days. They proved to be very amiable people, and in the short time that they were with us we learned to love them as a brother and sister in Christ. But I told him that for us it was not a question of receiving some individual families or members from the Liberated Churches, but of organizing groups of Liberated people into Protestant Reformed Churches. And I asked him, whether in the Netherlands, supposing there were a group of Reformed people that emphasized the theory of presumptive regeneration and wanted to become organized as Reformed Churches (maintaining art. 31),

the Liberated Churches would organize them and receive them in their fellowship on that basis. And both he and Mrs. Schilder replied that they would never do that. And I told him that we confronted the same problem here with respect to the Heynsian conception, *that the essence of the covenant is the promise and that the promise is for all that are born in the historical line of the covenant.*

"Nevertheless, it cannot be said that the declaration of principles is as such directed against the Liberated Churches, for they have not adopted any official conception of the covenant. At most, therefore, it should be said that it is directed at some of the Liberated, who teach that the promise of God is objectively for all the baptized children and that in this promise God is gracious to them all.

"It is true, of course, that due to the present circumstances the declaration of principles apparently devotes the lion's share of its contents to the question of the promise of God for all the children that are born under the covenant. Yet this is only apparent. The declaration just as emphatically denies the theory of common grace as adopted by the Synod of Kalamazoo, 1924. *It denies that there is a grace of God to all men, including the reprobate, in the common gifts to all men. It denies that the promise of the gospel is a gracious offer of salvation on the part of God to all that externally hear the gospel.* And it denies that the natural man, through the influence of common grace can do good in this world. And over against these points it maintains that *the grace of God is always particular and only for the elect, never for the reprobate.* It maintains that the promise of the gospel is not a gracious offer of salvation on the part of God to all men, nor a conditional offer to all that are born in the historical dispensation of the covenant, but an oath of God that He will infallibly lead all the elect unto salvation and eternal glory through faith. And it maintains that the unregenerate man is totally incapable of doing any good, wholly depraved, and therefore can only sin. Moreover, it repudiates the theory of presumptive regeneration and it declares that it must have nothing of the hierarchical action of the Reformed Synod of the Netherlands, 1939-'44, [these were two synods, Ed.] whereby they imposed certain doctrinal decisions upon the churches synodically. And whereby they deposed local officebearers. The only difference is that, whereas for the proposition that the promise is not for all the children that are born under the covenant, but only for the elect elaborate proof is furnished from the confessions, it was not deemed necessary to offer the same elaborate proof for the proposition that the Three Points are unreformed, for the simple reason that also the Liberated people are supposed to agree with us in regard to the denial of common grace and in regard to the contents of the Three Points."

So far the quotations. I did not highlight anything in this long quotation that was already discussed. Some sentences I italicised. Our readers can see that there is a new element here which has not yet been directly discussed. It will be worth the trouble taking a look at it.

Chapter 22
Concern

Once again we have to warn one another against poorly-considered formulations. The danger in this connection is not imaginary. Colleague Hoeksema apparently objects to the following statements:

1. the promise concerns *all the children* (that are born under the *historical dispensation* of the covenant, a terminology which I consider unclear or erroneous, but which I will not discuss now.)

2. *the promise of the gospel is a gracious offer of salvation on the part of God to all that externally hear the gospel* (let's say it this way: for all who hear it without ever accepting it: the reprobate.)

Those persons who would still accept statements 1 and 2 colleague Hoeksema calls importers of common grace theories (that is, if they are not careful). He does that aside from the controversy about Heyns, which means that we are still not finished with our clear *no* against the incriminated words of Heyns.

Now I believe that this is not correct. I have already rejected the word *concern* as being totally unclear. In its one meaning I accept it, in the other I detest it (see Chapter 14). So one of two things is true, either colleague Hoeksema did not reckon with the difference in the meaning of the word *concern* — or he *did* reckon with it. Then he thinks it is not allowed in any sense to say that the promise concerns all who sit in church. If this is his opinion, then this question comes up: how is it with those listening in church? Does the sermon count for all of them, yes or no?

Putting this aside we pay attention for a moment to the following statement: according to colleague Hoeksema one is not allowed to say that the promise is *a gracious offer for all on behalf of God*.

Chapter 23
Gracious Offer

If I understand correctly, his objection is that we should not say or suggest that there is any grace for a reprobate. Also receiving the promise of the covenant of grace is no grace for them. Nor is the sermon in any way grace for the reprobate.

Considering these things, one should bear in mind that colleague Hoeksema does not now expressly fight against the term *gracious offer*, also in regards to the individual who is rejected. The term *offer* was used in Kalamazoo and was rejected by Hoeksema (I believe rightly so). The objection is, however, valid without that term. In his opinion one cannot say that the reprobate in church have in common with the elect that the offer in the promise comes to them. The coming of *the offer* or the *promise* is a grace, so in this way, *inside the church,* they have a certain communal grace.

The result of this is that the *offer* of grace, the *promise*, is not a grace coming to *the church.*

If one would want to call it *"the historical dispensation of the covenant"* — this *historical dispensation* itself is no grace, at least not for all. Whether it is that for the individuals involved will have to become apparent — when we will see what the outcome will be in the future.

Apparently the aversion against the word communal grace is so strong that one is filled with fear of *common-grace-danger* with the arrival of everyone who, in whatever sense, would utter the statements 1 and 2.

Chapter 24
Supralapsarianism?

I believe it possible that supralapsarian motives are working here. We wish to say something about that. The question is: How does the Lord *value* the bare fact of the proclamation of the promise, the preaching of His covenant?

This question follows another question: how does God value the whole world, apart from sin? The creation?

The supralapsarian says: What God *does* last is *first* in His counsel. The last thing He *does* is to throw open a heaven and a hell. That then must be the very *first* thing which He *decreed*. Therefore the creation of that very beautiful world is only a *means* for reaching something else. Here lies the issue: the creation is *only* a *means*. It is not desired for and in itself.

But the infralapsarian remarks over against this: Stop talking from your exalted seat (which yet is so low) about

God and about the order of His decrees in such a manner that you lose the cohesion of the succession of His works. The creation of the world also pleases God in itself. The beautiful world is the work of His hands in which He delighted. Do not forget that. For instance, never say that God's *only* purpose with creation was to get candidates for condemnation along with candidates for glorification. Never say that God's intention with creation was exhausted with the fall of Adam as an occasion, opened by God, to generate for Himself condemnation candidates — wherewith the individual salvation of Adam becomes a side issue.

In these articles I do not delve farther into this matter.[19]

Although I myself do not want to be either a supralapsarian or an infralapsarian, I believe that just as God's disposition concerning persons from the beginning is determined by His counsel, so also God has a positive delight in His works. The purpose of the creation of a reprobate is not exhausted by saying: Look there, material for condemnation — his creation is *only* a *means* of *secondary* importance in contrast with the *primary* importance of God's counsel concerning the destination of the predestined (Coccejus).

I would also like to make the same point about the preaching of God's grace (along with His wrath), the proclamation of His virtues (love and righteousness), and the stipulation for His covenant-church (demand and promise). This preaching is always, besides the *means* for reaching what soon will be seen as result, a goal in itself; a beautiful spreading of God's name, a radiation of His glory, a prolongation of His early morning work in Genesis 1: giving man responsibility. God glorified Himself when He created men who were more than dumb creatures. He held them responsible immediately *by* Word and *by* covenant stipulation. This is the drama of history, not a temporary scheme soon to be thrown away, as people do with the wrapping of a good American cigar as soon as it is lit. No, this holding-responsible pleases God as proclamation of His

---

[19] More about this in my *Heidelbergsche Catechismus*, vol. III, final section.

praise. What about the individuals, then? We'll speak about that later.

Chapter 25
Apparently

We saw that the new American declaration wants to forbid the teaching that the promise *concerns* all. Colleague Hoeksema wrote that people who came into contact with the *mission* of his churches and expressed themselves in this way were only *apparently* willing to subscribe to the rejection of common grace.

Apparently.

If colleague Hoeksema is right, then we ourselves are checkmated by this *apparently.* We reject the doctrinal points of Kalamazoo along with him. We agree (in our way and with our own understanding of the word *concern*) with the people who met his *missionaries* that the promise concerns all who are baptized (in a lawful church). So also we are only *apparently* willing to subscribe to the rejection of those doctrinal points of common grace of Kalamazoo.

May we set colleague Hoeksema's mind at ease? We believe that our rejection of the common grace points, which he rejected, is consistently followed through by us. Not *apparently* please. If, along with this we calmly say that the promise *concerns* all (that is the promise, which for us is inseparably connected with the demand) then this is *not* in conflict with our rejection of the *points.* We believe that also colleague Hoeksema, when it comes to the point, and when the word concern receives its proper meaning, will teach "the promise concerns all." It is for that reason that we cannot admit that this is in conflict with our rejection of the points of Kalamazoo.

We will retract these words as soon as he openly declares, "My sermons in my church do not concern *all* who hear it." Those listeners might wonder about this as much as I do. But I do not yet believe that colleague Hoeksema would say this of his own sermons.

However, we must go on. We have to get out of this terminological mix-up. Is the promise (connected with the demand) not the main point in his sermons? In his sermons he will not, I hope, give a dogmatic treatise, but he will put his listeners under the judicial claim, the claim of the authoritative proclaimed Word, in the administration of the keys of the kingdom.

If we remember well, we once heard colleague Hoeksema say that the church does administer the promise of the covenant or of baptism equally to all.

Now, the church does *not* do that in its *own* name or on its *own* authority. It does it in the name of *God*, at *His* command. God does that through the church. That is what I call an administering of the promise (with the demand) to all, in the name of God.

I would not dare to say that this administration does not *concern all*, because then my sermon becomes a mere lecture.

On the contrary, the Catechism says that preaching is opening and closing, an official, valid act. The sermon is opening and closing by the administration of the Word, and the Word is the word-of-grace. The administration is one of *reconciliation*, and because it is that, its *threats* are *all* the *heavier* for those who neglect *so great a salvation*. In this unique indivisible entirety the sermon *concerns all*. God will not let Himself be mocked and will not mock us (Calvin). If colleague Hoeksema did meet Dutch or other people who separated the promise from the demand, yes, then the matter becomes different. However, in that case the people did most certainly not go through our school.

So the heavier the threat, the more drive to convert?

Chapter 26
Disposition

Now I come back to that supralapsarianism. Am I no longer allowed to call the official administration of God's word grace? A *grace* shown to the *church*? Is that the intention?

Preaching shows grace? ?

If so, then count me out on this point. I hope never to meddle with the proclamation of God's gospel (by an audible *and visible* sermon) as a work of *grace* by which He builds the *church* throughout all centuries, gathering and strengthening it. I call that grace. It is the handing out of a means of grace.

This does not prevent me, of course, from saying *no* to Kalamazoo (that American synod with its ill-considered conclusions, such as ascribing common grace ideas to the theologian Van Mastricht, which is something he never wrote). They alleged that God had a gracious *disposition* to all men, toward them all individually. I do not believe that. I am neither a supralapsarian nor an infralapsarian. I believe that the almighty God, all-wise, always knowing and searching and having all things in His hand, this God, Who in an ever ongoing continuation owns Himself, with all that is His (that is also His thinking, willing, deciding, destining, predestining) in equal intensity and perfectness, being Lord of Himself, always regards every man, the elected man as well as the non-elected man, with the same unchangeable, primordial and therefore also ultimative disposition. That is: toward one He is disposed as toward a rejected one, one whom He hates, not as creature but as a covenant breaker, a transgressor. Toward the other He is disposed as toward an elect one, one whom He loves as His favourite. However, I also believe that He reckons to him who is rejected and whom He causes to be born into the covenant a heavier guilt because he rejected the word of grace which he heard and by which God performed His service of grace for the building up of the church and for the salvation of that which was lost.

With this I maintain that the proclamation of God's great goodness and the administration of His gospel-word in the circle of the covenant is a means of grace and also a gift of grace which glorifies Him. For it is most certainly His work in which He is well pleased. I refuse to say, as the staunch supralapsarians do, that God has only secondary attention for His Own works which precede His *LAST* works (or God pays attention of a secondary degree to all historic works, minus the last ones — the opening of heaven and the closing of hell). I do not know of different degrees in God's attention for Himself and the works of His hands. Neither do I know of first or second rank valuation by God for His Own works or for His admirable workmanship.

At the same time I do say, that precisely because God's Self-glorification and Self-admiration are there to the full, also that of the proclamation of His grace, that the anger of God against the rejected whom He puts under the claim of the covenant, which also happened according to free election, is burning more fiercely (Canons of Dort, II, 5).

Am I no longer allowed to say, for instance, that the work of God for *the remnant of election,* of which Isaiah's prophesies are filled, is a work of grace? I believe it is. Still, I do not believe that this remnant, as meant by Isaiah, is the total sum of those elect to eternal life. There were also among them some who ultimately neglected so great a salvation.

Chapter 27
Beza on Decree and Execution of the Decree

Again we will call upon a supralapsarian to help us. People already know why I like doing this so much. I would like to plead that, to rescue the truth from the fixation of lies, we do not slap one another's ears if it is not absolutely necessary.

Well then, I choose Beza. He is called a supralapsarian and rightly so I think. Just read how he deals with Castellio. A few examples will allow us to know enough. He says to Castellio that he has to correctly consider that a *decision* must be sharply distinguished from the *execution* of that decision (of which Twissus also assured us). This, Beza says, is also true for the decree of rejection. The *decree* of rejection differs from the *fact* of *damnation,* the actual condemnation. To say it in Beza's own words: The cause of the DECREE is God's will (we would say good pleasure) but the *causes* (plural) for a person's damnation are lying in that person's own sin, in Adam's wilful transgression and in the conveyance of his corruption to us, in the fruits of that corruption. As far as the corruption is concerned, the "occasion and matter" of that lies exclusively in man. The counsel of God and our history with the end result therefore remain sharply distinct. When later Beza speaks about the order of the decrees of God then he is as *clever* as only a full-blooded supralapsarian can be. They can handle a lot. For example this question: Does the hatred of God for the reprobates precede the decree of rejection? Beza answers, O no, that hatred of God follows God's decree. Rejection is not an act of hatred, but an act of destination for that act of hatred. God, says Beza, destines for the act of hatred as many as He wills. The hatred itself comes later, after the decree. In the decree the hatred does not appear as present but as future (*futurum odium*). Not that the hatred of God would not be righteous. Far from it. There is a *substratum*, a substructure for God's hatred. All the material of this hatred is cleaving, inherent to them who are destined for perdition. Nevertheless no one should say — I am still quoting Beza — that God's hatred precedes the decree. Beza considers this just as absurd as it is to say that God already started hating when He still had to decide whom He would hate. God's hatred is no cause, but effect (see Beza, Tract. Theol. Genevae, 1682, ed. sec. i, 339-342, 347. Compare III, 432).

Now I do not believe much of that. The reasoning is not consistent supralapsarianism and there is too much fantasy. For instance fantasy about God, Who *still had to decide whom He would hate.* What is the word "still" doing here? What kind of reasoning is that about *before* and *later?*

However, that I do not agree with it is not what is at stake today. Many thought that Kuyper also was supralapsarian, even though he hammered on the term *common grace,* a term which is a typical infralapsarian thought. I have never yet seen a serious supralapsarian nor a serious infralapsarian. Because no one is able to maintain this system infra- as well as supralapsarians that is why they are making so many accidents in the construction of the *system.* When someone has fastened his teeth into what is not a serious *pièce de résistance,* he will presently growl to the right and to the left before he lets his titbit go. Then he will probably growl still louder. Maybe a soft reminder of what happened to others can help guard against this danger. Others, who were also supralapsarians, and yet . . . and those also who were infralapsarians, and yet . . . Well then, here is Beza, supralapsarian in format. And yet . . .

Yet, this same Beza writes several things that would not fit in the American formula as it apparently wants to be understood.

Chapter 28
Promise or Gift-Without-Strings Attached:
a Matter of Stipulation

Please take note.

Beza says, "If it says 'for the promise is for you and your children' one may try to save himself from the dilemma by making a very learned distinction between *promissio* and *pollicitatio*. This would allow one to say that *promissio* is a promise involving mutual stipulations (the one obliges the other, the other also the first) whereas *pollicitatio* would mean that which you, completely of your own accord, promise to another (without at the same time binding the other). It is better, however, to give up these sharp distinctions. The case here is about the freely promised goods" (not *promissio*, but *promissum;* not the act of promising, but what is promised). I do not ask whether Beza is right — I only ask this: If the supralapsarian Beza uses the word *promise* in this sense (I would nearly say in the sense so dearly beloved by the *Standard Bearer*), are then the people who met the deputies of the Protestant Reformed Churches in their mission-work and who say that the promise *concerns* all, you and your children, by this fact no longer to be understood in a positive sense? Just like our friend Beza? (Beza N.T. 1565, in Act. ii, 39).

Chapter 29
Beza About *Concern*

If it says "your children are holy" (1 Corinthians 7:14) then, according to Beza, they are declared holy as members of the church, in accordance with the covenant formula: "I am your God and the God of your seed." Does the covenant formula also count for the members of the covenant? Does it not *concern* them? What then does concern them? Please tell me. A dogmatic truth? Sure, that too, but the covenant formula is not a clipping out of a handbook for dogmatics. Let no one say that this holiness is an *effect* perhaps resulting from the *cause* of being in the church (that is, if the church would be blessed in the preaching). For then the supralapsarian Beza would interrupt, "Excuse me! Paul, in his reasoning, doesn't guess and look for possibilities, from cause to effect, but, just the other way around, he reasons from effect to cause. They are holy. That is a fact. They are included in the promise, that is also a fact" (*comprehendi in, they are included*). This *being included in the promise* is replaced in the following line by *being included in the covenant*. A remarkable expression for a supralapsarian, who in connection with accompanying matters didn't know how to keep himself free from conjecturing.[20]

Chapter 30
Beza About *Grace* and *Offer*

When Castellio, a fierce opponent of the Reformed, declares, "God loves all men," then this man selects, as usual, a few quotations from Reformed books, and says, "look here, these Reformed people themselves say that *grace is offered to all*." However, Beza says, "Tut, tut, don't read so hastily

---

[20] (N.T. on 1 Corinthians 7:14.) See further: *De Reformatie*, vol. 21, 84, in connection with the deplorable mistakes made by Dr. A. D. R. Polman in 1944.

and superficially. Why don't you tell us first, Mr. Castellio, what precisely it is that you understand by *grace*? You must know by now that some people call any *benefaction*, any *benefit* from God, *grace*. If you want to talk seriously with me, then you must understand *grace* to be reconciliation with God for free. Well," Beza continues, "I agree with the men from whose books you picked those quotations, that this grace is nowadays being offered to *all* people, in the sense that it is no longer to the Jews only, to Israel, as it was before. Race or rank doesn't count anymore in this case. It is offered *not only to the elect*, but *also to the reprobate. At least to many of them that are rejected*" (*plurimi*). Beza, the supralapsarian, says this (Tr. Theol., Genevae, 1582, i, 345.). Would Beza be accepted in the Protestant Reformed Churches? I would give the advice to admit him into the church; he wouldn't think of preaching heresies, nor is he doing away with *necessary distinctions*.

For, in one breath, he adds to his argument the words *quanvis contrario respectu,* which means, "in one case this offer is different than in another." This, however, addresses a more precise distinction. The main point for me is that Beza, concerning the *formula*, says with pleasure, "the offer is also made to all kinds of *reprobates*." One should not, in a mechanical reaction, answer, "this is in conflict with our formula, so it will not do." It may *do* or it may *not do*. It depends on your further *consideration*. And if the American formula wishes to discuss this with us then we will do so with pleasure. We don't want to do less than Beza in this more precise distinction. Neither do we want to be scared of this and scared of that and bound to formulas which forbid us to teach what Beza quietly teaches. You can never save anything with formulas. Beza speaks of an offer to various rejected persons and this has nothing to do with Heynsianism or with common grace theorems.

Chapter 31
Beza's Sketch

I made a note of several places: i, 203/4; 100/1; 171; 197/8; case Pighius 408; 413/4; 419; 687; iii, 432, 434, 416, but I fear that we are drifting too far off course. Let me suffice with a little from here and there in his *Brevis Explicatio* — his short explanation.

Explanation — of what? Well, of the sketch, which is nicely printed in Beza's book and which pictures the *summa* (the sum) of all Christianity. This print, this schematic drawing by Beza, is called by Heinrich Heppe, "the most complete supralapsarian representation of the order of God's decrees."

Heppe's print is not as nice by far as Beza's printer made it (Heppe, 119: Beza, i, 170). In any case the print is indeed something like supralapsarianism-in-etching. Beza gives a short explanation about this sketch (even though the matter takes the pages 171 - 205. These gentlemen of old could be so unbelievably smooth). We quote, in conclusion, some expressions from Beza's supralapsarian print.

For instance, when this sketch deals with the great question (aphorism 1 of cp. 3) of what the elect and the reprobate have in common in the *execution* of God's eternal decree (*in eo quod electis & reprobis commune est*), then Beza says, "God has devised a certain way which is common for elect and reprobate." Even more pointedly he says, "which is common to both, to 'the to be rejected' as well as to 'the to be elected.' He had to decree both under rebelliousness and sin (177)." That is point one (178). "He also had to create both in the position of righteousness." That is point two (178). "Over both of them came the *wilful* disobedience." Point three. "But in neither of these was God passive or idle." Point four (179). "God therefore values man's *wilfulness* on the one side, as well as His Own involvement on the other side, for, note well, not the salvation of A and the condemnation of B is God's ultimate goal, but 'His *glorification* and the *illustration* of it.' " Point five. "The guilt is, in both cases, only on the side of men." Point six (179, 180).

Chapter 32
God, Offering Himself

After this Beza starts dealing with the causal order in the publication and partial (*aliquatenus*) execution of the *election*. In this way we pay attention, among other things, to God's *offering-of-Himself* (*sui ipsius oblatio*; 181). We also pay attention to the *threat* (threat as a means to the realization of election! Have we, perhaps, forgotten this? [183]. We also read this in the Canons of Dort!)

Also the proclamation of the Law needs our attention (183). This too is a means in the gathering of the elect (183). The preaching of the law is strict (184). After that (*post*) follows the proposition of evangelical grace, but with the addition of a *condition* (does the *Standard Bearer* still always have peace with this? Peace with the supralapsarian Beza and his doctrine of a *condition as means for the execution of the decree of ELECTION*? 184). Someone has recently written against this, I think. This then was at the same time against Beza. However, Beza continues undisturbed. The added condition is *FAITH*! (184). Following this comes the powerful working of the Spirit with the Word (185). Only in this way do *all those things* (*haec omnia*) bear fruit, that is *also this threat* and *also this condition*.

Chapter 33
Condition and Threat

What Beza says is this, "If a church did not preach the *condition* and did not insert the *threat* in the preaching as well, then, what God has instituted as the means for the gathering of the *elect*, would be fruitless."

Would they now attempt to forbid us from teaching this, along with Beza? We wouldn't think of it, also not for the sake of peace, because *this* touches the *Canons of Dort,* concerning the *threat* and the *condition*; *promise with command!* (185). Beza's conclusion is that God gives *faith in order* that they could accomplish the condition, which was added to the preaching of the gospel (this condition is so inherent in all preaching, that without it *the sermon* is not a *sermon,* according to the supralapsarian Beza. Everyone should be careful not to be more supralapsarian than this king of supralapsarians). The elect are indeed going to accept the Christ offered (*oblatum*) to them (186). How was this Christ offered to them? "Well," says Beza, "universally and for everyone (promiscue)." Let me repeat the warning of before, both for our own and American use (186).

Chapter 34
Calling and Decree

Finally something needs to be said about the manner in which the decree of rejection is realised (190). We will only mention the following. In the case of adults God follows two ways, according to Beza (191). Some are completely excluded from the calling of the gospel. Even this *grace* they miss. Notice how the supralapsarian Beza calls the preaching *grace* although he remains far from the philosophy of Kalamazoo (concerning God's *favourable attitude* toward all individuals). *Others* — Beza continues — indeed are considered worthy (*dignatur*) to hear the preaching; *they are called,* but they are not willing and they cannot either. Yet, they are *invited* to the wedding feast (*convivium*), Matthew 22:2, Luke 14:6. (Does that *invitation* concern them too? I say "yes;" 192).

Among them God even has persons whose intellect He excites so that they believe, with a historic faith, what Scripture says (I will not discuss this term, Beza does not use it here either). Again, there are others — and they are the worst off — who have reached great height in order to fall the deeper (192). They enjoy certain (*quaedam*) grace, (yes, that's what it says, but Beza does not think of Kalamazoo), they march along in the church for a while, although they "return to their vomit," (1 Timothy 4:1, Matthew 12:43), "and fall away from the faith." God leaves them and the end result is hardening and blindness.

Now about the *calling*. We look once more at Beza's sketch. With the elect the calling is effectual. With the reprobate the call is sometimes completely absent (this concerns those who do not attend church and who couldn't care less, who do not know anything and whom the Word passes by completely). Sometimes, however, the calling is really present with the reprobate. It remains, however, without effect. This, according to Beza, is the situation of the reprobate who are under the preaching and received into church life. Apparently Beza knows of God both omitting the call as well as leaving the call sterile. In both cases he sees the result of God's hatred. Yes, for that he is a supralapsarian.

His little drawing looks as follows:

God's decree to reject those to be damned by their own fault

|

God's just *hatred* for those corrupt in themselves from the propogation of sin through Adam

| No calling | Ineffectual calling |

Spontaneous hardening

| Ignorance of the Gospel | Contempt of the Gospel when offered |

The last choice of words (bottom right) is not mine. Beza writes: *contemptus oblati Evangelii*. I would never draw such a picture. At the bottom it says: "O the depth of God's judgments! Who hath first given to Him and He will recompense it unto Him?

Romans 11:36" [*sic*! Romans 11:33, 35].

I fear that the complete sketch — this is only a small detail — is in a strained relationship with the mighty words underneath. This cannot hinder me at the present. With urgency I'd like to ask our esteemed colleague Hoeksema, "Would you not assist in removing this declaration from the table? I cannot imagine that you would tell your missionaries: When a certain Beza comes, put this declaration before him, and, in case he refuses, let him go." I myself would refuse, colleague Hoeksema, whereas I still believe that I am Reformed and that you have a grand task in that great America. Your churches will forfeit your opportunity if they will bind in such a way that the Bezas, though supralapsarians, are sent away. What then will happen to those poor, gentle-looking infralapsarians?

The issue is Supralapsarism

Chapter 35
Summary Regarding Beza

Beza says "the gospel is *offered*," but he is against Kalamazoo. I take it upon myself to prove this. Beza says "*the call* comes to *all*," but he is against Kalamazoo (to all who are incorporated into the congregation, for instance).

Beza knows of a call with two kinds of *effects* (I do too), but he does not know of a calling with two kinds of *contents* (I don't either), for the *calling is not a dogmatic aphorism*, but a *demand-promise, promise-with-condition*. One person can presently fulfil this condition, thanks to God's grace, thanks to grace alone. The other will never fulfil this condition. However, *all* are placed before the *condition* (in the covenant). I consider this to be Reformed, and I also consider this a basis for *preaching*, rather than a popular, easy to understand lecture or a treatise on camouflaged fate.

The calling (vocation), according to Beza, is the ordinary *service of the Gospel* (iii, 434). It is *the voice of the Gospel* sounding in church through the service of men. This one voice will have different effects also in the church: not every heart of stone will be softened. And the reprobate? Beza says things of them which some nowadays don't even dare to repeat, "also to them the doctrine of salvation is offered" (*sibi oblatam salutis doctrinam*). This offer, meanwhile, is no Kalamazoo-product with Beza. Just look at his grim sketch which first shows *hatred* and after this the calling, which has no efficacy. But Beza also recognizes the authority which lies in that offer (iii, 434).

I conclude that our liberated people may strengthen colleague Hoeksema's ranks in his struggle against the doctrine of common grace which makes victims en masse in America. If, however, he thinks that they, with their statement that the promise *concerns all*, still *might, without knowing it, accept common grace*, then he is mistaken in their and in our intention. He can see in Beza, that they are not caught in the nets of Kalamazoo. It is up to him to help them and by it to enrich his own church life. I prefer them in the church rather than a group of men who say yes and amen to everything that is presented to them.

Common grace? I don't read anything about it in Beza, but I do read about *common misery.*

Chapter 36
Addition Concerning Beza

Before we continue our theme we would like to make an addition to what was said in the foregoing chapters. We have already shown a little detail of the sketch which Beza has, in the form of a drawing, inserted in his Theological Treatises. Our readers will know by now what our intention is. One of our ministers mailed an excellent photographic reproduction of the same sketch to us which we reproduce on this page; it was not in the way Beza presented it with all the words in Latin, but it was a Dutch translation.

Some marginal notes may be useful.

a. This reproduction is, in its impact, not comparable with
    the original of Beza. On one half of it Beza's headings
    are connected by thin lines ornamented by flowers and
    angel-figures, on the other half there are, for instance,
    snake-heads and demon-heads. But in this way one
    does get an impression.
b. It is not a complete impression, however. Some of
    Beza's words are omitted, for instance, in the heading
    (description and *division* of causes). Also omitted are
    the three texts: top left: Romans 9:21 (Hath not the
    potter power over the clay, of the same lump to make
    one vessel unto honour, and another unto dishonour?);
    top right: Proverbs 16:4 (The LORD hath made all things
    for himself: yea, even the wicked for the day of evil);
    and at the bottom: Romans 11:36 (O the depth of God's
    judgments! Who hath first given to Him and He will
    recompense it unto Him? This is actually Romans
    11:33, 35).
c. There are still more points, but we leave them for now.
    Only one thing we consider to be of importance for
    the "American" issue. Beza, the supralapsarian,
    acknowledges a calling on condition and says that this
    is *no common grace* at all. Just look at the right side of
    the sketch. Hidden behind this public *earnest* calling
    divine hatred can be concealed.

Would I say it in the same way? That is not the point
here. I only ask, "would you refuse to accept Beza as a
member of the church in America?" We would thankfully
accept him here, although we would like to reflect
theologically upon his constructions, on the one construction
as well as on the other.

Chapter 37
Preface to the *Staten Bijbel*

In addition to what has been said we could make some remarks concerning those *conditions* in the covenant, with which we, for that matter, will soon be finished (I dealt with it somewhere else in greater length and we cannot always keep repeating things), in reaction to what colleague Hoeksema writes in the *Standard Bearer*. Some remarks I will leave until the conclusion. This time I deal with only one single point.

Our readers will remember that concerning those "conditions" I referred to the *preface* of the *Staten Bijbel* of the New Testament. In this preface we find strong words about God promising eternal life *on condition* of faith and repentance. Colleague Hoeksema says, "O.K., it is in the preface of the *Staten Bijbel*, but what does that prove? It has happened before that apostasy has arisen shortly after a good and strong synod. Couldn't that be the case with the *Staten* Translation? Don't bother me with this *Staten* Translation, even if it is delivered by the same synod that rejected the Arminians, but rather come with the *confession* itself. Is it in the confession? Let the confession speak as to whether mention is made of conditions in the covenant. If not, then I don't accept this word."

I do not believe that either colleague Hoeksema or Dr. J. Ridderbos would really pass off the *Staten* Translation with a shrug of the shoulders. Those who prepared it were no children nor far-off descendants of the Synod of Dort. Indeed, the whole *Staten* Translation bears the mark of conscious, pious, and necessary resistance against all Arminianism.

Chapter 38
Must an Opinion Literally
be Found in the Confession?

Colleague Hoeksema says, see above, that we should ask whether an opinion is found in the confession, not whether the *Staten* Translation expresses an opinion. The main point is whether one may require such confessional proof when receiving men, such as emigrants from the Netherlands, into one's own church community? Does one have to say, "Your own opinion must be specifically worded in the confession, and if not, you will not be admitted by us?" I don't believe a word of it.

God is not a collector of dogmatic, symbolic, confessionally balanced people. Rather, He is the God of the *living* and not of the *dead*.

If the Reformed church of Kampen would have accepted me, the undersigned, K.S., as a confessing member only after I was balanced in the sense described above, I would never have been accepted. I believe that I only became a bit wiser in symbolics and confessionology after I received a teaching mandate in Kampen and thereby obtained time for study.

I also believe that the consistory of Kampen *rightly* admitted me, not on the ground of my confessionological ability, which wasn't there at all, but on the ground of the fact that I heartily desired to live according to the confession and on the ground of my promise to submit myself willingly to the discipline of the church *if* it would appear that my views were not in keeping with the honestly explained and interpreted confession.

This is how I would consider our emigrants. Colleague Hoeksema has received from God the prominent grace and the *enormous calling* to be a salting salt and a shining light in that wide America. This is an *enormous* task. I travelled through the vast width of America and I saw large areas without a trace of a Reformed church. I often thought of what a task it is to represent the church of Christ here. I see

in the church quite a few men and women who are not a whit
wiser than I was when I made profession of faith. I consider
it a privilege to be allowed to gather them together and adjure
them "For God's sake, don't *increase* the *number* of *churches*
any more than it is already." When I see them coming, one
chased by a socialistic wind, the other by fear of communists,
the third by famine, and they would ask me, "Am I *allowed*
to praise the Lord in your church, which I acknowledge,"
then I would not demand, "Submit to an *examination*, so
that we can determine whether the theological terms you use
are the same as the formulas expressed in the confession."
In other words, "Can you repeat from memory the lessons
learned by heart." Neither would I say, "Come in, good man,
never mind the confession."

I would ask them, "Does what you are teaching come
into *conflict* with the *confession*?"

In that case and only in that case should we talk, for the
confession is not a piece of doctrine-in-extract, but an
expression of what is *necessary* for a Christian to believe.

Now, if colleague Hoeksema agrees with this, and I
believe he does, for he also has been led through grievous
ways, then I would limit myself strictly to this question (in
the above mentioned case), "Is your opinion *in conflict* with
the confession? If so and there is proof of it, when reducing
the basic question to the confessional contents, then I should
have a serious talk with you. We are not an open field, but
the church of Christ." I would not ask him, "Is your opinion
stated in so many *words* in the confession?" I would try to
remember that the confession is older than my
contemporaries and that it only notes what is necessary as a
form of unity.

Well then, if colleague Hoeksema wants to ask, "Is the
doctrine of *conditions* in conflict with the confession?" then
we would be moving forward. Then I want to tell him, "I
will undertake to prove that the *one* doctrine of conditions is
in *conflict* with the confession, while the other *one* is
completely in agreement with it."

Chapter 39
The Better Question

In connection to what was pointed out above, we remark, "If someone asks to join the church, and, after having been invited there unto he explains what he thinks about 'God and divine matters,' " then you may not ask him, "My good man, is everything you say *literally present* in the confession?" If he is a parrot, who can only imitate, or a person who nods *yes* to all questions (which is worse), thinking that those questions are business for *theologians* only, then he will not be an asset to your church. If he is not a parrot, but a *man*, who *has* something, then watch him closely and put him through his paces. He will be one of two, either a great gain or a great danger. Put him through his paces well, but don't ask him whether his own words are formulated in the confession. Just find out whether they place themselves *in line with it* or whether they *go against it*.

Maybe he has something new that can help you or motivate you to a more discerning thinking. Maybe he does not have anything new at all, but only a more defined formulation of the old.

Chapter 40
An Example

Take ourselves, for instance. Several weeks ago (*de Reformatie,* no. 6, Nov. 11, 1950) we raised some objections against the fact that someone, in 1950, would state in a new formula that election would be called the only *cause*, or fountain of our salvation. This so called, to say it again, newly stated formula would be over against imagined or real heresies of *contemporaries*, and would pretend to be used to cut off new or revived old heresies by a sharper formulation. One might ask, "But is this danger not imaginary? Don't the Canons of Dort (I, 9) also say that election is the *fountain* of every saving good?" And that from that (*unde* — "that" can mean: a. that *fountain*, or, b. that *saving good*, or, c. the *fact* that election is the fountain of every saving good) proceeds faith, holiness, and the other gifts of salvation, and finally eternal life itself, as its *fruits* and effects?

Certainly, that is what the Canons say, and for that reason I mentioned right from the start that we will not bother him who uses this expression as such. We say no more than Calvin who calls election the *foundation* and *first cause* (C.R. 51, 147), although he of course knows and somewhere writes that *foundation*, clearly defined, does differ from *cause*. Calvin can handle the Sorbonne.

However, if one starts binding and accentuating that expression and pinning it *down in* a *new* binding, then we say, "Excuse me, it says *fountain* or *spring* (*fons*), if you want a more precise distinction, it means something different than *cause*. Look up Gomarus, for instance, (to name one of many and certainly not the weakest brother) in the index on his works concerning the idea of *cause*. When making more exact distinctions you will see how he states some very precise meanings; meanings which sometimes have nothing to do with the idea of *causa*, as it is applied, for instance, in the doctrine of causality."[21]

Although it is not even found in the confession of Dort, I have nothing against the word *fountain* and not even against the word *cause*, as long as I have the freedom to say what I, more precisely speaking, want to have understood by it. From this it will become apparent whether I concur with the contents of the confession.

---

[21] *Causa notatvel argumentum et rationem probationis: quae causa consequentiae; vel argumentum essentiale, cujus vi res est, nempe efficiens, materia, forma, finis.* This has quite a number of possibilities. We continue: *causa e efficiens* (!), which even, *metaphorice pro occasione rei antecedente* (think of the doctrine of the *aphormai*, or *occasiones*, in the struggle about supralapsarianism!) *Causa impulsiva est vel efficiens, quae synecdochice causa impulsiva dicitur, vel finalis. Causa per accidens accipitur proprie, cum praeter intentionem efficientis aliquod ab eo fit, improrie, per metath. pro occasione tantum antecedente. Causa per accidens dissidiorum, excaecationis non recte dicitur Christus.*

But one should not tie me down to a *more precise statement*, binding me to a very limited definition of the term *cause*. If this is done it may be that one who uses the word has a *wrong* opinion of its meaning and comes into conflict with the *contents* of the confession. Yet he who rejects it (exactly by doing so) will defend and safeguard the *contents* of the confession against misconception in times to follow.

This is only an example, which I give on purpose, because an interested and valued brother approached me about it. When Calvin speaks of God as *fons* then I will sign my name under it, as long as he speaks about it loosely. But when Plotinus does it, I say with Calvin, "Thanks, but I will never sign that."

The same can be the case here.

It is not proper to trip one another in precise binding formulas for one word. It is only proper to ask whether a word, used by a contemporary and properly explained, is consistent with the old confession as a form of unity; otherwise we scatter the church, which God gathers, with 'theologians' sticks. This happens sooner than desired. Just look at the misery of Kalamazoo in 1924 and of Utrecht in 1944.

Chapter 41
Conditions and *Dort*

I see a slight symptom of this danger — don't read more into my words than it says — when colleague Hoeksema says, "that preface to the *Staten* Translation appeared after the Dort synod, but it has happened more often that after a good synod apostasy arose. This argument doesn't tell me — Hoeksema — anything." If colleague Hoeksema wishes I can prove to him that *already* in the Written Conference, which means *before* the Dort synod, the Reformed party spoke of conditions in the covenant. If he wishes I will show him that also the acts of the Dort synod themselves repeatedly speak of conditions, and that it fought fiercely against any doctrine of conditions whenever it was understood in the sense of Arminian thinking (that faith and repentance were taken as the ground or moving *cause* and last or *first* cause of election; or, that God was made dependent on free-will-equipped-men for whom He politely had to wait, *looking* to see whether the man would be so kind as to believe).

But also that those *Acta* speak quietly and cheerfully of a Reformed condition-doctrine, that God does not give the one without the other. Meanwhile He is the fountain, the merciful Disposer, and the Giver of the one as well as of the other. This is then again connected with the fact that He addresses me without giving any prediction concerning my future but all the more binds me to His promises which never come to me without demands.

Chapter 42
Conditions and Canons

It is thus that on the one hand the Canons of Dort (I, 9) *condemn* every idea that election came about on account *of foreseen faith* (!), or the obedience of faith, or any other qualities as the *cause* or *condition* in the *still to be elected* man (*eligendo, gerundivum*), while on the other hand it is confessed (I, 10) that the cause[22] (within God's own depths) of election (the decree) *is His good pleasure*. Election does not consist herein that God, out of all "possible" conditions (nominalistically), has chosen or selected certain qualities or actions of men as conditions for salvation. There it speaks of God's decree; and that decree is *free, completely free*. He elects and rejects without being bound to anything. He elects unconditionally and *He also rejects* unconditionally. Maybe the last mentioned point is often forgotten in the heat of the struggle, which in my opinion is fought rather weakly by some.

---

[22] Again we find an example of a possible change in terminology in order to maintain the idea of what was confessed before. Here again we find the word *causa*. This word was properly used in the days of Dort. But when later on pantheistic philosophers made it necessary for the Reformed to give a more precise definition, the objection to speaking, for instance, of God as *causa sui*, grew stronger in Reformed circles.

But the same confession *also* says that the *promise* (!) comes *with* (*cum*) the *command* of faith and repentance.

From election, which is hidden, unconditional, and completely free, we turn to God's *speaking* and *addressing*, in which He signifies or pictures for us to *what end* He has elected us and the *way* by which the elect *come to* and are *assured* of salvation. It is God's *freedom* that He does not give B without A, C without B, and D without C. However, once He has instituted the sequence between A, B, C, D, etc., then we are bound to it in reverent acknowledgement that He still remains free, also, for instance, with little children whom He, in His decree, calls out of this life before they know how to distinguish an A from a B, a B from a C, and a C from a D.

It has been *His* free will, for instance, that a man who desires to marry not only may but must say, "I will not become the father of a child unless there is a woman who desires to be its mother, for that is the *condition* which God puts before me and He *promised* Adam that the human race would be multiplied *under this condition*." Does this man limit God in His *freedom*? *Not* in *any* way! If he is Reformed he knows that God is *able* to call a son, Who has no *father*, out of Mary, and that God is *able* to generate children out of *stones*, whether He takes *dust* out of the early paradise soil, or stones from the Jordan Valley — He *is* free. I am not allowed to say that He, in His *choice,* and in *His* choice, is bound to any condition in the multiplying of men. Christ in the desert knew *very* well that God was able to generate children out of stones, and *bread* out of stones. The devil then also says to *Him*, "Do it; isn't it *good orthodox theology* that God is *free*, that He can unconditionally do what He wills?" But Christ said to Satan, "Certainly, *He* is free, but I am not! He commanded me, *as an obedient Human being,* 'Man shall not live by bread alone, but by *every word*,'" which means, that time and again there is the added condition which holds for all men the authoritative command of God. This command contains blessing and power unto salvation.

That is also the case here.

Chapter 43
Details from the Canons

The same *Canons of Dort*, which want nothing to do with conditions for salvation being chosen out of a set of *possible* conditions (to which God would be bound; I, 10), have nevertheless acknowledged that God in freedom *decreed* that ordinarily salvation will not come as a fruit of his election without faith preceding it (I, 12). These fruits are pointed out in the Word of God. Herein comes the promise with the command.

Not *before it*, so that the command comes dragging behind.

Not *after* it, so that the promise comes limping behind.

It comes *with it*, so that both as one entity come marching directly toward me. Only in the unity of the two, inseparably connected, have I met my *God* and not an *abstracting theologian*. He came in such a way that I can know that I met Him. He *said* to me, "I come to you speaking in this manner: promise *with* command, command *with* promise (II, 5).

Thus, within the circle of God's *speaking*, the promised goods are bound to the *condition* of accepting those goods.

Is this idea Arminian?

Nonsense, also this accepting is *given*, *also this is* contained in the promise.

Is it Arminian to say: I will receive a watch on the condition that I do not get a bunch of loose little screws, sprockets, and springs?

A condition for something is that it is not divided into parts or fragments. A condition for the evening is that it must have been morning. The condition for salvation is the salvation of my faith. The condition for A is A. The condition for everything is all that is contained in that everything.

Conclusion: there is *no meriting* condition (I, 9).

It is *not* one of a series of possibilities to which God should be bound, from which He would make a choice (I, 10).

It is *no* prerequisite condition which would bind God (I, R. of E., 4, 5; I, 9).

It is *not* a changed condition (I, R. of E., 7).

It is *not* a contingent condition (I, R. of E., 7).

Yet it is a *designated* condition (I, 12; II, 5) *to which I am bound*, as Christ was in the desert, and as was the man who wanted to become a father according to the ordinance freely set by God.

As the Bible says, "*those who honour Me I will honour.*"

It is only a little trick to say, "this is an Arminian idea."

It is a smaller trick yet to say, "this is Heynsian."

Yet it is plainly biblical, although I know that *every Arminian minister* would *preach* with pleasure about this text.

But what it boils down to is this: A PROPER DISTINCTION.

My advice to all and to myself is that we do not get hung up on any *theology*. There is no *liberated* theology, neither is there a *Protestant Reformed* theology, although a classis speaks of it with a frankness I fail to understand.

Ask me whether what I say is in *conflict* with the confession. Don't ask me whether what I say is literally in the confession. I take it upon myself to prove that much of what is written in the *Standard Bearer*, much like what you will find in my own books, *is not in the confession*. It is, however, still thoroughly Reformed, and is therefore, when it comes to the point, in essence stated *in* the confessions. Just as the *Reformed* doctrine of conditions is *essentially* in the confessions.

Chapter 44
Character of the Promise

In what we read in the new *Brief Declaration*, which was recommended from Protestant Reformed side to be accepted by the next synod, the description of the character of the *promise* caught our attention.

It is denied that the *promise of the gospel* is a conditional offer to all who are born in "the historical line of the covenant," that is to all who are baptized. Over against this it is stated that *the promise of the gospel is* "an oath of God that He will infallibly lead all the elect unto salvation and eternal glory through faith."

In order to properly evaluate these statements, which means to judge them in a proper way, the negative as well as the positive one, we should look at the Acts of the Synod of 1924 of the Christian Reformed Church, which was so foolish as to standardize a few ill-considered and awkward points to which they wanted to bind Reverend Hoeksema by subscription. He refused to do this, and rightly so. He was then deposed on account of this good service for the protection of the sheep from a wrong use of the rod. A lesson should be taken to heart by all of us and also the present Protestant Reformed churches, so as not to fall into the same fault of binding people to new doctrinal points which are not clearly defined, not consistently and logically built up, and above all do not in a most simple and clear manner render or clarify what is already found in the confession.

Allow me to remark that I am not *convinced* that the rendering (in the *Brief Declaration*) of what the synod of Kalamazoo has stated in its "Three Points" is literal. If it is not, and I fear that I am not mistaken, then that would already be an objection against acceptance of the *Brief Declaration*. When I quote my opponents in official points I have to do it literally.

For that reason I am not dealing with the question whether the *Brief Declaration*, concerning the character and significance of the promise of the gospel, does indeed deal point by point with (or opposing) the Three Points of Kalamazoo. Do Kalamazoo and the *Brief Declaration* essentially touch each other? If not, then I believe that also for outlining the position over against the Christian Reformed people and for the historic illumination of the courageous fight which colleague Hoeksema really fought and was forced to fight, it is better to put this *Brief Declaration* aside, as it is not a true picture of the thetical and antithetical position.

Chapter 45
Promising is *Saying*

And now we go on. We are speaking here about the *promise of the gospel*: of *the gospel*.

If I understand only *one* syllable of the *gospel,* it is that it has to do with *messages,* not with God's hidden thoughts, but with what He has to *say* to us. In this case it is not spoken by an objective reporter who can produce news of facts and *happenings*, but by an ambassador sent by Him. In front of others, such an ambassador represents his own king with authority. He does not just come to tell something about His majesty, such as when and where he was born, what his family tree looks like, how many children he has, where his residence is, what his habits and hobbies are, in short, news that fills our papers and magazines — numbers and facts. Not so *this* ambassador; *he* comes with official authority as an accredited representative, to do business. He comes not to refer to a truth, but to say, "This and that is the will of my King. I am appointed to make this known in His name. I do not bring a news report and I do not just communicate facts, but I bring an authoritative word concerning a testament."

This is the way things are when we speak of gospel-servants as ambassadors of God.

Chapter 46
Saying with Authority

In short, when I read of the promise of the gospel then I stick to this leading thought (compare my *Heidelbergsche Catechismus*, vol. II, in which some grounds are given for this). I want to read this term *promise of the gospel* as it is used in the Canons of Dort, especially in II, 5, where we can read that the promise of the gospel ought to be announced (this is something different than reading the heading "City News" in the newspaper) and proclaimed (this is something different than giving an objective paraphrase of it) with the demand to repent and believe. I would love to see the Canons of Dort maintained.

They frankly say:

a. The promise comes with the command. This is not a mere news report, mere objective, "hm, hm," but a placing *under God's claim*. No news-cast, such as: apples don't fall far from the tree, or: it is nice weather, or: the earth has two poles, or: God is a simple Being, or: three persons are together one Being, or: a heaven and a hell are coming.

No dogma, no mere statement, but an official address to someone, an approach. An announcement. A proclamation! (*Proponere*). Don't be a proponent of yourself or of your sermon proposal. For *that* proclamation of *your* word has nothing to do with the Canons of Dort II, 5. The preacher must officially present God as the Promiser and Commander in one, in one authoritative message!

When in bygone days the herald of the Kampen City Hall announced and proclaimed from the balcony of the City Hall something in the name of His Majesty Emperor Charles V, then this was quite different from what the local bulletin reported about His Majesty, or from what the mayor told his wife in the evening, such as how many jokes His Majesty had told (if that was the case . . .).

I choose these *strange* examples on purpose. I like to show people the difference between a dogmatic *statement* about God and an official *address* in the *name* of God.

b. The Canons also say that this promise-with-command has to be declared and published [or: announced and proclaimed] to all nations, without distinction, to whom God out of His good pleasure (according to His fixed decree) *sends* the gospel (II, 5; Added is *promicue*, communally, collectively; without discrimination. No covenant-collectivism or something miserable like that. Yet, homiletic annunciative collectivity).

c. They (the Canons) also say that this announcing and proclaiming has to be done *earnestly*. I read this word *earnestly* apart from the unfortunate paraphrase of Kalamazoo, and have written about that extensively. People should not group me with the common grace sinners, for I am not going to sit in that corner. One should also not wildly conclude that this is Heynsian; you should not combat Heyns unless you point out *what* is actually wrong, otherwise this man becomes a myth and that is fatal for the church.

I read the word *earnestly* in the Canons *and I leave it there.* That is what I also *confess.* God earnestly *shows* in His Word (*ostendere*) what is pleasing to Him (this is therefore a message) and He *earnestly* promises to all who come to Him and believe Him rest for their souls and eternal life (this *is* a promise). An *earnest* statement conforming to an *earnest address.*

Well then, on *this particular issue* the subject is *stuck*, if indeed anything is *stuck.*

Chapter 47
Earnest

They may keep the word *well-meant* as far as I am concerned. To me it sounds too much like a tea-party conversation. However, I will not give up the word *"serio"* (earnestly) to anybody and I believe that colleague Hoeksema thinks the same, for he also wants to maintain the confession. He appeals to the confession and that is exactly why we are attracted to him. I find in the word *serio* more than the Kalamazoo-friendliness, more than the discovery by two Dutchmen (J. Ridderbos and K. J. Kraan) of the always bountiful God. I hear in the expressions *serio ostendere* (earnestly pointing out from the Word) and *serio permittere* (earnestly promising in the promise of the gospel) also *the flaming wrath of God.* The earnestness of Emperor Charles V in the days of the imperial visit, differs from the complacency of Kampen's mayor when in the evening he told his wife (a bit subjectively) what kind of man this emperor was. "*Serio,*" says the emperor, "I decree." *Serio* the emperor grants these and those privileges to the city of Kampen. He says, "be careful and do not act as if nothing happened today." Indeed, they *are* careful, these aldermen!

Well then, just as Emperor Charles V did *not* hand a *news-item* to the city of Kampen stating that in his empire such and such customs existed and that such and such ideas were milling about in his imperial head, but that he *serio* granted a *promise-with-demand*; so, in a much more exalted sense, it is with God, the King of Kings. When He seriously addresses me through His ambassadors He does not show me a bit of dogmatics. He *does* something to me. I can never get out from under it.

Chapter 48
What Kind of Oath?

I come back to the *Brief Declaration* and ask, "What are you doing with the word *oath*?" I read there, "The promise of the gospel is an *oath* of God." Using a distinction of the fathers, is this an oath of assertion (which confirms something) or an oath of promise?

Is it an oath which says something which is a fact with Him, or an oath which promises and pledges something to me?

I say the latter, although I do not exclude the *assertoric* aspect of it. For indeed, God has stated how it stands with Him. With Him it is this: It *pleases* Him when I come to Him. He takes *delight* in it. I *don't have to* think, no, I am not even *allowed* to think (for then I reject what He seriously has reported about Himself), that if I come He will still consider whether it pleases Him, or consider whether it can please Him. Look, *that* would be *Arminian*. He has told me (reporting facts about Himself), *Quisquis*, when *anyone*, even if it is a prostitute, a publican . . . even if it is one . . . as miserable as . . . I myself, comes to Him, then this coming is pleasing to Him. He delights in it. If I do not believe this, I stand on the same level as someone who does not believe what the gospel has further revealed. Even if I do not exclude the *assertoric* part yet, the *promissoric* part comes first in His *oath* which He *swore* to me. He says something *not only about* all people which are this or that, but He says something *to me*, not just a *statement*, but an *address*. He calls my name; He says, "You there," and then He calls us by our name.

Chapter 49
An Oath of Assertion of a Common Truth?

Do I find this back in the *Brief Declaration*? It says, "an oath of God that He *will infallibly lead all the elect unto salvation . . .*" etc. If it does not say more then I say that this is not sufficient. This is dogmatic. This is a news report. It is also not in agreement with the Form for Baptism. This is a stating of facts *about* the total number of the *elect*. What I need is an *address* to me. In the promise of the gospel I do not receive a dogmatic lecture about God's usual dealing with the elect, for even the devil can tell me that, and he doesn't for that matter doubt for a minute that God indeed leads all the elect in the manner mentioned here. I want to hear something that was addressed to me when I was earnestly called.

Chapter 50
About the Elect, or *To* the Called?

I do not say that it is done on purpose and I hope that by careful consideration the misunderstanding, if it were threatening, can be taken away. However, to be able to meet each other again on well known ground I like to point out this fact, the *Brief Declaration* says that the promise of the gospel is an oath *about* the *elect*, but the Canons of Dort say that the promise of the gospel is an oath *to* the *called* (III/ IV, 8). The Form for Baptism says the same. I will stick to the Canons and would like to say to all emigrants and non-emigrants in America and here [in the Netherlands], "You should do the same!"

For I repeat what I wrote years ago against Dr. J. Ridderbos and his synod, "The figure of an unconditional offer of salvation for the *elect* is fiction. It doesn't exist." There is, however, a dogma about the elect. But that which God announces as a promise, that which He promises, is not unconditional, but is, in the sense of Ursinus, a conditional promise to the ones who are called. Those who come and believe hear in that promise the promise of the infallible guidance to salvation as certainly as God says now presently in addressing them. He will honour those who honour Him by their coming, but he who despises Him will be lightly esteemed. Exactly this *with* that other was the earnest annunciation-proposition of the King of kings.

However, it is not only *about* those who are *born in the historical dispensation* of the *covenant* (what is that, *a dispensation?*) but, for instance, also for the Ethiopian court-official of Acts 8. As far as the baptized are concerned God has *underlined* the oath with them. He has underlined it with a *heavy* line. Confirmation of the sermon which contained promise with demand, but *not a new gospel*. Neither a gospel supplemented with a newly added paragraph. No, the *old* sermon, heavily underlined, with a sign and seal added. The *certificate* remained unaltered as far as its text was concerned. Only now it was provided with a seal — presented to me.

Chapter 51
Quality and Address of the Oath:
Two Central Questions

Earlier we promised to speak about the Form for Baptism.

We concluded that the American declaration asserts that the promise of the gospel is an *oath*. An oath concerning God's infallible dealing for and in *all the elect.*

The fact is that *all the elect* can only be pointed out after judgment day in heaven. We can never do this here on earth.

In so far as the American statement speaks about this *oath* of God, the conclusion from this accepted position must be that God swears this oath to a large group of unspecified people.

Maybe you say, "This is not true, for the oath is spoken through the service of the Word *in the church*. And the church is a community which can be pointed out."

Certainly, certainly, but because of that we first asked, what kind of oath, assertoric (reporting facts), or promissoric (giving promise)? Doesn't the service of the Word do more than promise only? It also proclaims facts. For instance that Christ came to this earth. That once the earth will perish. That there has been a flood. That Abraham departed from Ur. That Christ will return. Nevertheless *those facts* are never *separated* from the service-of-promise (God doesn't tell stories). But there is a difference between an announcement for everyone who wants to listen to a publication of facts and a penetrating into the the life of a *specific person*, with the sharp sword of promise-with-demand.

Therefore we just asked: *What kind of* an oath? Now we ask, *To* whom *is* this oath given?

Does God audibly, that is audibly for church and world, speak to an *unspecified address*?

We say, no. Oh, yes, He can thunder a statement from on high, over our heads. But, please permit me to share the image which comes up now: He does not baptize via a loud speaker which proclaims a recorded general message over our heads. No, He comes down from the pulpit, stands right next to us and says, "Mary, name and surname;" "Cornelius, so and so, I baptize you." He does not say something about a multitude which I in this life will never see, but He says something *to* a *specific person*, who has a name and family-name.

Chapter 52
To *Will*

Of course the American theologians who have drawn up the *Brief Declaration* know this just as well as we do. I presume that they took this into account when they formulated this statement. There is a small word in the sentence we dealt with which reminds us of the Form for Baptism, the form with which the Lord indeed descends from the pulpit and says something to little Mary and to the little Cornelius. I refer to the small word to *will*. The American statement reads, "That the promise of the gospel is an oath of God that He *will* infallibly lead all the elect unto salvation and eternal glory through faith."

The small word to *will* is from the Form for Baptism. The American authors of this *Brief Declaration* have remembered this very well, for they fiercely opposed Heyns who dealt very extensively with this small word to *will*, which — we repeat — did not always seem correct. I fear that also the exegesis of the *masjaal* (parable having a hidden meaning) of *the Vineyard* (Isaiah 5) must have created misunderstanding because an exegete may never lose sight of the never-to-be-neglected difference between a masjaal and a dogmatic statement. We don't have to tell what the parable is. It reads as follows:

My wellbeloved hath a vineyard in a very fruitful hill:
And he fenced it, and gathered out the stones thereof,
and planted it with the choicest vine,
and built a tower in the midst of it,
and also made a winepress therein:
and he looked that it should bring forth grapes,
and it brought forth wild grapes.
And now, O inhabitants of Jerusalem, and men of Judah,
judge, I pray you, betwixt me and my vineyard.
What could have been done more to my vineyard,
that I have not done in it?

wherefore, when I looked
that it should bring forth grapes,
brought it forth wild grapes?
And now go to;
I will tell you what I will do to my vineyard:
I will take away the hedge thereof,
and it shall be eaten up;
and break down the wall thereof,
and it shall be trodden down:
And I will lay it waste:
it shall not be pruned, nor digged;
but there shall come up briers and thorns:
I will also command the clouds
that they rain no rain upon it.
For the vineyard of the Lord *of hosts*
is the house of Israel,
and the men of Judah his pleasant plant:
and he looked for judgment, but behold oppression;
for righteousness, but behold a cry.

This parable has also often been discussed in America. With Heyns it returns repeatedly, also in writings and other documents which are unknown in the Netherlands, but which I glanced through while in America and which, in my opinion, were not always correct. However, what sensible man would for that reason say, "When Heyns says something you always have to go the opposite way?" Watch out for reactionary-theology. The discussion has often been confused. One said, "Do you see that? God was *willing*, but this vineyard was unwilling." The other said, "If it comes to the point, God was not *really* willing, for when it goes wrong with us, then this is all decreed in His counsel, and if He *wills* something, *really wills* it, well, then it will happen!"

I believe that both opinions are wrong; the one forgot that this is a *parable*, and the other forgot it just as well. The one dealt with the parable as with a page from a *dogmatic* treatise, and so did the other.

The discussion has, however, brought forward some good. If you read the parable for what it is, the conclusion has to be that the prophet says to the church, "Promises were given to you, labour was bestowed on you by the permanent administration of God's covenant Word, with the prophetic pastoral care, but you did not *believe*. And God is going to do with you, what He *told* you right from the *beginning*: 'He, who rejects Me will be rejected.' Covenant-breaking is to be followed by covenant-wrath." Therefore we read in the Form for Baptism that we receive a promise, but it goes together with a demand (two parts in each covenant) and thus the promise does not come to unknown *elect*, but to those *called* by name and surname, who *are included* in the *covenant community*.

Chapter 53
To You

When the Form for Baptism declares that, by baptism, God makes promises to us it clearly says, "He makes promises to *this by-name-mentioned*-child." He can safely say this and also teach this to us, because the promise goes hand in hand with the demand. To *this child* is said, "You, child, under the condition (that is to say under emphasized assurance and stipulation) that your faith will be and must be the only way in which all this will happen (therefore you are called and *obliged* to this), the Father *will* provide you with all good and He *will* avert all evil or turn it to your benefit, the Spirit *will* impart to you what we have in Christ." Here we do not turn away from the area of dogmatic expressions. However, we are *personally* addressed by the magistrate (God) Who summoned us to the *City Hall* (see also my *Heidelbergsche Catechismus*, vol. II). Also there you don't follow a scientific objective *lecture* about the law, the civil code, philosophy of law, or something like it, but whether you are educated or uneducated, you are simply *obliged* to something.

Chapter 54
Are, or also *Become?*

That is why we just said, "It doesn't say that already for a long time, before baptism, or before we were born (for instance by God's creator-rights upon 'all men,' or by the fact that He established a covenant with Adam in Paradise) we were obliged to a new obedience," although all that is mentioned here is also true. But it says "therefore are [Dutch: *worden* = become] we by God through baptism, admonished of, and obliged unto new obedience . . ." This is not an *assertoric* oath that the Reformed course of ethics was well grounded, but through baptism it is a *being obliged* by a promissoric oath in an occuring judicial act to the service of the Lord. This took place at the *same moment* in which we were marked with the claim of the promise.

Chapter 55
Conclusion on this Point

We may conclude that not only the *Canons of Dort*, but also the Form for Baptism teaches us that the promise of the gospel is not an *oath* that God will lead all the elect to a destination (although this is all true) but an oath *to* a specific person, that He wants to lead this specific person, *called* by name, to the final salvation.

If someone calls this Arminian, I would quietly say, "It is not, and you do not understand the situation." How often doesn't the Bible say, *If? If?* I rather find myself again in agreement with Dr. J. Ridderbos, from the good time, when he still wrote commentaries: "The promise of Zachariah 3:6, 7 is a *solemn assurance* (no dogmatic report, I say) and *contains a promise, connected with a condition*." I would like to ask, "Can Dr. J. Ridderbos not be admitted into the Protestant Reformed Church?" Watch out that you do not become like him in casting out, or obstructing. We did not cast him out, but he cast us out. We will not persecute him for that little sentence; but he persecuted us when he allowed this sentence to be attacked by himself, to take away the key of knowledge — not the Kuyperian but the confessional knowledge — when he wanted to hinder candidates, elders, and ministers from entering the kingdom (of service).

He did not succeed, but he couldn't help that.

Chapter 56
God's Reliability at Stake

We will probably not be mistaken if we presume that the *Brief Declaration*, printed at the beginning of this booklet, thinks that only by the stand they have taken the *reliability of God* can be maintained. What the precise scientific description of this would be we let rest for now. Even the scientifically uneducated understands immediately what it is about, when we read, "And God surely fulfills His promise. Hence that promise is surely only for the elect."

You see the reasoning:

a. God fulfils what He promises.

b. Only to the elect He fulfils the promise.

c. Consequently the promise is only for the elect.

We are not going to repeat that *is for* is an unclear term and that the oppressive question remains for each church member who asks, "Is there anything promised to me which I can consider as having been spoken to *me* personally?" We have dealt with this already.

Something else demands our attention: *God's trust-worthiness, God's reliability*. Such a syllogism (= logical conclusion) is so very appealing. It seems so simple. It is as clear as daylight. But, is it?

Chapter 57
The Dangerous Art of Syllogism

What if I put up another syllogism which is also simple? For instance like this:

a. God fulfils what He threatens.

b. Only in the reprobates does He fulfil the threat.

c. Consequently the threat is only for the reprobates.

Can you say anything against it? One shouldn't say, "Oh, yes, threat can mean threatening with temporal chastisement, which is meant in a fatherly way and in this way also the elect can be included, because they are most certainly chastised paternally." No, now we are speaking about the threat of eternal death. It seems to me that this syllogism is just as logical as the one of the *Brief Declaration*. However, then the question which I mentioned a minute ago as oppressive, oppressive for church members who are not allowed to contradict it, becomes even more oppressive. As I said before, such a church member must keep asking, "Is anything *promised* to me which I can accept as *certainly* having been spoken to *me*?" I can add to it now that this church-member also can go on asking, "Am I *threatened* with something that I can accept as certainly having been spoken to me?"

There we are.

For in both cases it is about the reliability, the veracity of God.

And now, one of two things is true:

Either they acknowledge, that in church, in the name of the Lord, the members of the church receive promises and threats;

Or they say, "No, although the Lord addresses us by name and surname, He only delivers a dogmatic speech and a person is not addressed with a *personal promise*, nor with a *personal threat*. For whether they will be *carried out to him* has yet to be seen. If his end is not good then that person had apparently never been *promised* anything."

We timidly ask, "Was he then perhaps *threatened* with something?"

Chapter 58
Uncertain Baptism

When one says, "yes, certainly, for when he is traveling in the wrong direction, it appears *after* the fact that the threat indeed was directed to him, that it indeed did concern him." Then we respond, "Then the threat was conditional? *Why then not also the promise?*"

"No," they will say, "it was unconditional, only nothing was said concerning whether or not the threat or the promise concerned *this person.* For God fulfils all He says unconditionally (thus also His threat). With baptism we receive an unconditional promise and an unconditional threat." When twenty or thirty children are baptized at the same time you can secretly think that perhaps among ten, twenty, or thirty the Lord has made a difference. But what when only *one* child is baptized? Then you say, *"you can never know exactly whether* (without mentioning a name) an *unconditional promise* was given today, or (without mentioning a name) an *unconditional threat* was expressed today."

With this view point what are they able to say with certainty about what will happen, not only about what is *presumed* to happen (in America they are also against presumption, they do not presume the one or the other)? What are they able to say about what is *in reality* a certain and *confirmable* fact with baptism?

Here in the Netherlands I do know it. I maintain, "that child is given a promise and a threat *at the same time.*" The child knows, "I may and must accept the promise, I do not stand at a distance as one who is kept far outside the door." The *Canons of Dort* tell us that there are also those who are kept outside the door. But I don't know how they can ever get out of this difficulty when they state that the position of the *Brief Declaration* is exclusive and when they forbid it to be contradicted.

Chapter 59
No More Threat?

But perhaps the promoters of this declaration say, "No, no, not at all. There is no threat in the church of the New Covenant, there are only promises." Then I no longer know how to read the New Testament and I no longer know what I can do with the Canons of Dort.

In the New Testament the threat is very clear, even stronger than in the Old Testament (for instance Hebrews 12:25, and other places). In the Canons of Dort (V, 14) we read that the Lord begins this work of grace in us by the preaching of the gospel, with the command of faith and repentance, but He maintains it with (among other things) threats. Thus they have a fixed place in the preaching and accompany the administration of the sacraments.

So, there we are, and the debate began with the question of how God's truth or veracity, in which we all believe, is to be related to the difficult matter of baptism.

The one says that God keeps what He has promised, for He is reliable. Others say that to some baptized persons the promise is not fulfilled. In that case I would *conclude directly about God* that He did not promise anything, although He indeed *did say* something to the baptized person.

Someone who speaks in this manner means it honestly and we understand him; he wants to maintain God's reliability. He must come to the conclusion, I can only maintain God's reliability when I say, "You, baptized one, hear something promising said to you, but be careful — it may not apply to you." Then I ask, "would that indeed be God's truthfulness?" I don't understand it. Still, I would say to them, "Teach it in that way then. At least then you are clear, even though, in my opinion, it is totally wrong."

Chapter 60
To *Conclude* About God, or About Oneself?

Wouldn't a person who comes to a conclusion so hastily want to be careful for a moment with his hasty conclusion? We just said that he directly concluded about *God*? I would suggest there is another way; you can also conclude about *yourself.* You can also reason as follows:

God keeps His promise, God also keeps His threat, for He is true. To some baptized persons the promise is not fulfilled, but the threat is. To others the threat is not fulfilled, but the promise is. Now I conclude about *myself*: did I perhaps come to a conclusion about God too hastily? Namely that He, to the one (without the man hearing it) has *promised* (?) something, but what the man indeed was able to hear (because he was called by name at his baptism) He did not keep, namely as far as it sounded promising? Would I not have to conclude that *every* covenant contains two parts and that therefore God to one and the same person has given promises and threats? But then in this way, that the grace of God which was administered, not as something strange, but as something that has been granted to the church, was taken as basis, also for the measure of our punishment?

The one concludes: God is true; He actually did *not* promise *anything* (to the reprobate person who was baptized).

The other concludes: God is true; He actually did not promise anything without the threat (and this concerns everyone who is baptized).

Chapter 61
Isaiah About God's Truthfulness

Now I am able to read again the famous text about God's truthfulness, Isaiah 65:16. When the Lord God has judged those who rejected Him (verse 15, forensic) and has given a new name to those who were faithful to Him (forensic, compare Revelation) *then* they will swear by *the God of truth.*

The God of truth.

That is the God who keeps His promises and His threats and who has never separated them.

That is why I am afraid for the ghost of an inaudible promise in a not audible form, and this also goes for the threat.

They come to us *audibly, together* and *at the same time.*

I am afraid of a fictitious story: the unconditional promise, which is not audibly spoken to a named person, but which does use audible language, for instance in a Form for Baptism.

I am not afraid of an audible word which connects both. For that is "serious."

And as long as the Lord *keeps us*, we also will maintain both of them.

I have never yet understood how someone can say, "When someone who is mentioned by name is baptized God says to him, 'To you I promise,' but sometimes this person does not believe — in that case nothing was promised to him."

But it was said to him, wasn't it?

Thus that saying did not mean anything. What counted was what God *thought.*

Is that the proclamation of God's truth? God indeed *said* it, but you cannot count on what God *says*? He perhaps *thinks* differently from what He *says*? I believe that this view does not do justice to God's truthfulness and *paralyses* the preaching, also the preaching about this matter.

Chapter 62
Provisional Closing Remarks

As the reader has already understood, we are coming to our provisional conclusion. *Provisional,* for one should almost never say that one will not say another word on the matter. Doing so would be dangerous and certainly not always in the interest of those to whom you wish to render a brotherly service. When these articles are not understood as such a service one does not understand our intention.

But I thought this will be a *closing* for the time being.

I admit that this is a change from my original intention. It seems to me that there is more in the *Brief Declaration* worthy of close consideration. Indeed, originally we had intended to have a close look at the whole document, because it seemed to me that the matter was worth dealing with for the interest of our churches as well as for the interest of the Protestant Reformed Churches, whom I came to know, and to love (I still do). I respect them for their manly struggle in the days of the binding on the matter of common grace which was carried through in America in such an awkward way after a limping report with all kinds of theological derailments. I also have respect for their work among our emigrants on whom they spent a great amount of money, their warm love for members in need and the diaconal work for our churches right after the war (something we shouldn't forget, they dried many tears when we, here in the Netherlands, were without clothing and food). They received in colleague Hoeksema a man whom I continue to keep in high esteem and consider to be my friend. In the latest issue of the *Standard Bearer* he assures me that I am still his friend and attests to our mutual friendship, of which I readily and gladly take note.

I recently received several letters from America, also about the matter of the well known *declaration*, and this time I intentionally did not answer these letters. People should never be able to say that I tried to drive a wedge between colleague Hoeksema and the brothers who were always united in heartfelt love with him. I openly declared my opinion about this declaration when it appeared to be publicly necessary. For the rest I wait quietly to see what will develop on that side of the ocean (or what will be destroyed).

*   *   *

The fact that I now provisionally stop finds its reason in an article from the *Standard Bearer* of February 15, 1951, which I received by airmail. In this article colleague Hoeksema begins to write something about my series of articles concerning the *Brief Declaration*. All right.

If he had dealt extensively with them, or had announced that he would we would probably have continued and given an overview of his answer with a response from our side. But what appears now?

This is what happened: colleague Hoeksema says, "several points of Schilder's articles are not *to the point*," which means that they do not *touch* the *point in question*.

I am not at all angry about this. When you are debating in the press you know ahead of time that you can count on something like that.

But in this case I feel like saying, "Alright, if that is what you think I had better stop."

For those who see the *point in question* as I see it I have said enough, I believe, about the *Brief Declaration*. The fragmentation and divisions which have been made in Canada indeed prove that there are people, both supporters and opponents, who see the *point in question* exactly as I do. As for the others, who see this issue differently then I do, my writing will not help at all as long as they put the *point in question* where they now put it and where it really is not: in this case you can talk endlessly but it will not help a bit.

For the *point in question* is *not* whether Hoeksema, or Heyns, or Schilder, or Petter, or whoever else, is a *good dogmatician*. To tell the truth, that wouldn't matter to me a bit in this issue. I see dozens of questions about which no one either here or there has a rounded off theory. And I do not like a church of clever theologians.

The point in question is only this: may you dare to *break a church apart* for a dogmatic formula of Schilder which Hoeksema can attack, or one of Hoeksema which Schilder can attack, while indeed both in good conscience subscribe to the Three Forms of Unity. Both are also prepared, if need be, to answer questions concerning their doctrine, not on the basis of a freshly tabled formula, but by rendering a clear account, by going to the root of the matter. Both may stand amidst a crowd of brothers and sisters, who have learned to say: do not divide the church by academic wisdom which harps on one point and overlooks another point which is just as true. Or: who uses a word with which you can go in two or more directions. Or: who draws a dogmatic line, which neglects another one. Or: who by creating diagrams is turning away from Scripture and confession.

If colleague Hoeksema is of the opinion that for me *the point* is whether the *Brief Declaration* is a *dogmatically* responsible document, I have to answer, "No, my friend!"

For me *the point* was this: here, for instance, is a person, K.S., who will not sign the *Brief Declaration*. He is prepared to give you a hearing on all points. If necessary he would challenge you, just as he challenged Berkouwer and Ridderbos, to point out even one Arminian tendency or opinion in it. He can assure you in advance that Hepp didn't succeed in it, that Berkouwer did not and that you wouldn't either. No one will. Next to him are many others, whether or not you cited them (not always completely fair, I believe), and when you found a sentence which seemed inaccurate in your view, then these men were suddenly presented as heralds of the continuouing doctrine of the Liberated Churches (which is not the name of our churches[23] by the way). They don't want to be such heralds any more than I, even though what they wrote further proves that you didn't draw out of their sentences what in the broader context was contained in them or must have been contained in them. Leave all these men with their phrases alone for a while — even if their name is Veenhof, Bremmer, Churchill, or Poincare — and take now, just once, as an example one of the deputies for contact with Churches abroad, who has objections against making the *Brief Declaration* binding and has made it very clear that he could not possibly be convinced to promise not to teach or to propagate anything which does not totally agree with the *Brief Declaration*. He would also refuse to promise this if he would perhaps move to America. This is the fine

[23] The churches of which Schilder was a member were called (before and after the Liberation of 1944) *De Gereformeerde Kerken in Nederland* (The Reformed Churches in the Netherlands). However, since two federations of churches in the Netherlands officially have the same name they are often identified as (synodical) and (liberated). Since "liberated" is not part of the official name no capital "L" should be used as is often done in books and periodicals. — Ed.

point: would he — seeing this refusal — be accepted as a member of a Protestant Reformed Church, about which my colleague Professor Holwerda, in the well known letter, has written such very nice and glorious things (please, do not forget that)?[24] Could he become member, yes or no?

None of you should say, "fine, for that one, but for the other person, no!" No one should say: "Your explanation may perhaps pass, but those from someone else or from that other person cannot really be tolerated by us." No, leave all explanations alone. Only take the *bare fact* that one of us would not subscribe to the *Brief Declaration* (arguments don't count) or in any case would refuse to promise not to work against the *Brief Declaration*. Can they become members in full right, yes or no? *That* and that *only* is *the point.*

If you say, "No, they cannot become members because I bless the decision of Classis East, which asserted, 'One must promise not to teach anything against it,' " all right, then we are finished. If this would become a general opinion with you, fixed in a decision of general synod, then we know where we stand. But I would pity your churches with such a decision, for I am firmly convinced that by such a decision you would commit ecclesiastical suicide as soon as you do such a thing. As churches of Christ in America, you have a great mandate, and in times past you were also enabled thereto, for your churches have accomplished beautiful things. You would have gone too far as did the Dutch synodocrats, about whose deeds you also have publicly declared that you do not want to have anything to do with. For your churches would have made the admittance to the pulpit, to the baptismal font, and to the Lord's Supper table dependent on a dogmatic declaration which one can, I am

---

[24] In the *Standard Bearer*, Vol. 25, Aug. 1, 1949, p. 470, Rev. G. M. Ophoff published a private letter of Prof. B. Holwerda to an immigrant in Chatham, Ontario. In this letter Holwerda advised this immigrant to join the Protestant Reformed Churches since Rev. Hoeksema's conception of the covenant was not binding in the P.R.C. See about this letter also Gertrude Hoeksema, *A Watered Garden* (Grand Rapids: Reformed Free Publishing Association, 1992), pp 149-154. — Ed.

convinced, contest without ceasing to be Reformed, also on the points on which it was contested. If in the capacity of a *dogmatician*, who in that capacity has nothing to do in this case, you ask me privately what I think is the better course of action — to *fight* this *Brief Declaration* or to *tolerate* it — in order to keep the Reformed confession, following the line of, let us say, the *Canons of Dort*, then I say, we must do the *former*. That is than my dogmatic opinion which is, for that matter, based on a confessional one, although I do acknowledge you in your endeavours, also to be faithful to the confession.

If you say, "Yes, among you liberated people there are persons who indeed can become members with us, *without* this promise, because we do differentiate; we would admit brother A, although he refuses to sign, but we would not admit brother B (and the brothers C and D, etc.) because we have read some phrases of what they have written with which we do not agree and thus we would have to have a talk with them first," then I say that your *Brief Declaration* has received the deathblow as a *binding* document. For if you admit that even one person in the world can refuse to listen to the opinion of Classis East and thus can refuse to promise to teach nothing against the *Brief Declaration*, and that that person can nevertheless be allowed membership with you, then you have abandoned the whole *Brief Declaration* as a binding piece, as a shibboleth of doctrine, which is to be maintained according to the Scriptures. Then you have said that apparently you must be able to *discuss* it once again with the people. Well then, I, K.S. say: "Good, talk it over and lead that discussion back to what the confession says. But put this *Brief Declaration* in the archives, for then the matter has again returned to the *existing* confession."

As you can see I speak precisely to you as I did to the Dutch synod in my peace-making (indeed!) letter of December 13, 1943, and I would earnestly like to advise you to please listen to it, as we like to listen to you, for they are all familiar sounds, and let's learn from the history here in the Netherlands. Here we also have some who, swept along by some sort of passion, have said, "What letter of

December 13? The man should bow; go on, go on, continue to bind!" Now they deeply regret it even though they don't admit it verbally and although their propagandists (Visser and Norel to name only a few recent ones), out of thankfulness that this letter also wanted to guard them against the ramrodded synodical decisions which they now deplore, now accuse those who wanted to protect them in time when they were not awake yet. Sleepers often blame those who were on guard in time.

So I maintain that my discussion was indeed *to the point*. You said, "If you consider the promise of the covenant in the way of the Liberated you teach 'common grace' within the community of the covenant." I pointed out, "Pardon me, but look at Beza, a supralapsarian just like you, colleague Hoeksema." I said, "Beza contradicts your *Brief Declaration*; yet he is a supralapsarian and for that reason welcome to you. Even he does not believe *common grace* within the circle of the covenant à la Heyns — please be careful with the cliché *Heynsian,* just as we have to be careful with the cliché *Kuyperian* — for Beza teaches that God gives promises with conditions also to those whom the Lord has predestined for hatred. I leave this construction for what it is, but my question, "Can Beza become a member with you?" is certainly *to the point.*

If you say, "that is not the point" then I say, "I had better stop." Not out of anger, but because the readers should hear something different. If one pushes the matter off the table, then the reader regains his rights.

If you say, "The *Brief Declaration* is according to the confession" (which I denied, with references to the declarations and the ecclesiastical literature around Dort, before, as well as during and after Dort) then I say, "I had better stop, for I cannot continue repeating myself."

If you say, *Heynsian* while I was writing, "mention the fine point, for on the point *well known to me* we contradict him and for the rest neither Heyns, nor Hoeksema, nor Schilder, nor Bavinck, nor Kuyper, nor anybody else is completely good, or totally bad, but what counts is the confession," then I'd rather stop.

If you say, "Faith is not a *condition*, but a *means*," then I say, "I had better stop." I maintain, "means are also conditions," and I have shown that too. The means is the condition for reaching a goal.

*   *   *

Allow me, nevertheless, with this provisional ending, to add one kind-hearted word.

You once more referred to the letter of colleague Holwerda and to our conversation with the ministers Kok and De Jong. I wish that you would let that matter rest. For:

Primo: The brothers Kok and De Jong only said good things about you and about your churches. Only good things. Only good things!

Secundo: No plotting took place with anybody, and they said very clearly that they were not here in any official capacity. Neither did they ask, "Are we allowed to come?" We asked them. Just as we would ask anybody who happened to be in our country while we were meeting together.

Tertio: They did say, and I consider this an honourable testimony, also for you, that we can learn from one another. That was also exactly what we found in your own letter. They also said, "Don't think that we swear by every opinion of any person, even if he is a highly esteemed brother or a beloved pastor." Really, I don't understand at all why someone in America can be angry when someone says, "You are not bound to the opinions of this one or that one." Of course this does mean that you are bound indeed to the confession and therefore also to all opinions which one or other person teaches which *conforms* to the *confession*. But for the rest, isn't there a text in the Bible about knowing in part, about a still deeper penetrating into the mysteries-of-salvation, yes or no? Of course, you say, no one among us doubts that. Well, the ministers Kok and De Jong didn't go one step farther; nor did we, who have had some very pleasant conversations with them.

And Quarto: When colleague Holwerda (with whom I have not spoken about this article) tells a man, who asked him for advice, "Those churches are churches of Christ," isn't that a refreshing cup of cold water, after all the revilement which has come upon your head and that of your churches? I once thought that I understood something of the misery of that foolishness and worse which was brought upon you in those days of Kalamazoo. I do know something about that, I believe. Should not an expression like this cause rejoicing? I myself was glad when I read it.

You may say, yes, but Prof. Holwerda also wrote: Hoeksema's opinion is not binding in every respect.

Let me speak for myself in answer to this. From certain sides *they* try to create the impression that the undersigned is a kind of prelate in the church who just sticks to his own point, who gets angry when contradicted, and only wants to have things his own way. Such nonsense makes me angry. I prefer to say clearly that I think it is a venomous attack when they say: "K.S. gets angry when they don't share his opinion, and he does not want to hear people say that it is not binding." On the contrary, and I know it, Holwerda says that the liberated churches wouldn't be liberated if they were bound to the opinions of so and so. K.S. too is only a man, like Hoeksema, or Ophoff, or Kok, or De Jong, or Petter. After we die others will start arguing. The young Ridderbos wrote about us: "They well-nigh canonize Greijdanus." However, he could have read in the same paper articles stating opinions which differed from those of Greijdanus. Yet none of us wants to diminish in any way our high esteem for him and his work. As long as I am around I will use the right to argue. Let them contradict my arguments. But I think it a pestilence for every church, and therefore I call it a pestilence from the side of our opponents, when someone says, "There and there you are not allowed to say anything against so and so's opinion." I would consider it an honour if someone would write about my *churches*: Do not think that there you have to echo what Seakle Greijdanus, or Benne Holwerda, or Cornelis Veenhof, or Pieter Deddens, or Hendrik Jan Jager, or Klaas Schilder, or Douwe van Dijk, or whoever else may have a name, says above the confession: You may freely contradict K.S. for instance. With the myth of a black and white diagram and with vicious gossip of "This one and that one are church-monarchs, *salva pace* K.S., they have brought enough misery upon us already." I think that colleague Holwerda, in saying this, has *honoured you* and *your churches*. I would also like this to be admitted openly for once, and an apology sent to those who were included in this for-me-completely-incomprehensible-matter, and who, one by one, were as innocent as little lambs.

You have a broad task in America; I believe, however, that you are being led to a dangerous demarcation line. If the *Brief Declaration* is accepted you have made a turn which is fatal. It would be even *if* your *Brief Declaration was completely right*, which is not the case, in my opinion.

Finally, at the same time I am informing our readers that you have advised us that you have reserved a seat with the boat departing on June 24 for your trip to the Netherlands. You add to it, "That is, if they still want to see us and if they still desire correspondence in spite of our doctrinal differences."

I do not want to be responsible for your not coming by binding our longing for a conversation to *conditions*. (!) You know what our deputies have written. You also know that I have no knowledge of doctrinal differences between your and our churches. Your *Brief Declaration* is not definitely accepted yet and you can still avoid a great deal by saying, "Don't accept it, and certainly not before we have carefully discussed it also in the Netherlands." You know particularly well that *your deputies*, and thus also among them *yourself*, have said, "*dogmatic differences* are not yet *confessional differences*." You know that a formula which is declared binding and against which no one is allowed to speak, receives somewhat of a confessional value; a binding *interpretation* of the confession. I deny that the fathers of

Dort would have interpreted the Canons in this way. You also know that if you definitely accept this document you would say *before* you arrive here that "also you, deputies, cannot become members with us."

And now it is up to you.

Our deputies have written to you, and the editor of a magazine [Schilder means himself, Ed.] doesn't see a single reason to reconsider what he wrote and yet wants to be a good friend of yours and of your churches. He does have reason to say to you, "If *you* come, and if *you* still desire to see us," although we clearly say, "we will not sign your *Brief Declaration*." We know very well what it is to be Reformed. So, don't make obstacles *when God does not compel you to do it*. Not in your conscience, but in His *Word*.

I am convinced that the God Who sees the number of His confessors diminish by the month, does not approve of His American sheep being bound to the *Brief Declaration*. One can contradict it as an Arminian and as a Pelagian and as a semi-Pelagian and as a crypto-Arminian and as a thousand other things. But — one can also contradict it in the way of the undersigned, and the undersigned believes his thinking to be Reformed. Till now you have not convinced me otherwise. It is up to you to say to me and to the others who think like me, "Perhaps you are a good fellow, or maybe a very bad one, but — you cannot become a member of *our* church." You will not hear such a judgment coming from our mouth. We learned our lesson in 1944, and we mean it when we say to you what we also said to Ridderbos and Polman: God has more patience with the church federation than you do, if, before you go on the boat, you accept the *Brief Declaration*.

One more little question: "How many serious members of your churches, whom you wouldn't want to miss for any money, understand your *Brief Declaration* in all its detail?"

Chapter 63
Correspondence

The deputies, appointed by the general synod of Amersfoort, have provisionally decided in their latest meeting to bring the state of affairs concerning the Protestant Reformed Churches in America to the attention of the churches. They very much wanted to submit their report to the churches in time, but, as will be evident from the following letters, they are not able to establish the date as they please because of the possibility of an American visit to the Netherlands. Nevertheless, they wish to inform the churches concerning the state of affairs. The only option which for now seems desirable and possible concerning this is to present the correspondence as far as it has developed until now. Its motivation follows from the contents of the documents themselves.

What follows here is the correspondence:

Zwolle, January 29th, 1951.

Deputies for Correspondence with Foreign Churches of the Reformed Churches in the Netherlands.
Address: Corn. Jolstraat 56
Scheveningen, The Netherlands

To the "Committee for Correspondence with Foreign Churches" of the Protestant Reformed Churches in the U.S.A.

Esteemed, Reverend Brothers,

In our meeting of January 12th, 1951 we received notice of your, gratefully received, letter of August 3rd, 1950. We established our answer in our next meeting of Jan. 29, 1951. For the time being we can restrict our answer to a request, the compliance of which could perhaps shorten the correspondence considerably between you and us as deputies.

Our request is this:

We learned with gladness that your Synod has decided to delegate "you to the Netherlands, as a 'Committee,' with a view to conferring together with us." We believe along with you that verbal contact between you and us can only be beneficial for the task delegated to us by our Synod, as it was beneficial for the understanding and appreciation of your churches and people when we met two of your ministers whose presence in this country we made good use of to get to know each other.

We read that the deterioration of *international circumstances* resulted in the fact that your intended visit in 1950 could not materialize. It is now your intention to visit the Netherlands in June or July 1951. It is also part of your plan to remain a few weeks in our country, with the purpose of attending the sessions of our own General Synod at Kampen, to be convened August 24th.

It is this last communication that leads us to our request to hasten your coming to the Netherlands as much as you possibly can. We think about the fact that your Synod meets during the summer, and that in your churches, even from those closely connected to your committee, pressure is exercised to accept officially and definitely at the next Synod of your churches a declaration, which, one of the members of your committee said, was *certainly very necessary* for "maintaining the *purity* of doctrine" (*Standard Bearer*, xxvii, 4, 61). If this would happen, then this fact would undoubtedly be of great importance for the relationship between your and our churches, because this not yet accepted *declaration* is already serving as a working hypothesis and has created an expected rebound by members of *your* churches and of emigrants who were or still are members of *our* churches. If you would arrive in our country after your Synod has taken a definite decision concerning this *declaration*, then we as deputies, taking the decision into account and also its eventual results, would have to prepare and finalize our report to the Kampen Synod with the greatest care and would first have to have had the opportunity to carefully consider what the situation is, a situation which would have thoroughly changed in several important respects by such a decision. No one knows what results such a definite decision would have, especially since this *declaration* itself has already been established as a working hypothesis. Even you yourself, sojourning in the Netherlands, would not be able to verify the state of affairs as changed by such a definite decision. Reporting to our Synod would be made difficult, and a decision of our Synod would be hampered. You would sooner be faced with a decisive fact than we. Your decision would not only have been prepared, but also have been taken *in the period in which we were still conferring with each other*, even though that decision is of such fundamental significance for the consultation and for the eventual conclusion. Maybe *so* much that in some respects the relationship between your churches and our churches, especially in light of a possible new *binding* (a binding prepared by your churches and brought to a conclusion during the period of our deliberation), would change, a change which could be called a *Copernican* change.

It must be clear to you that we consider it of utmost importance that the meeting, to which we gladly look forward, takes place as soon as possible.

The more so, because we read in The Report of classis East (*Standard Bearer*, Nov. 1, 1950) that your classis East spoke officially of a Protestant Reformed *doctrine,* and also of Protestant Reformed *theology,* and that this classis has decided that, in its opinion, a consistory has to require persons who ask to be admitted as members to be educated in this doctrine and to be required not to agitate against this theology.

This report puts some questions before us as deputies. Some time ago we read with gladness the following words,

"We stand with you on the foundation of Scripture and the Three Forms of Unity and maintain the pure, Reformed church-polity, being averse to all *hierarchy*" and that "*dogmatic differences, which possibly exist between you and us, are not confessional differences.*"

At that time we realized that in this, in our opinion, your position was rightly based solely on the *confessions* of your and our churches. At this time, however, we are placed before the fact — in the period of mutually started contact for deliberations — that one of your classes officially, at least in its *propaganda*, speaks of Protestant Reformed theology to which they wish to bind prospective members who seek admission.

We as deputies do not know what Protestant Reformed theology is, but if the classis (which apparently does know what it is, and judges that consistories and members know what it is) might be of the opinion that the mentioned declaration is a clear rendering of this theology on one or two of the hundreds of points which are around in any *theology,* then we put over against it not only some question marks concerning the picture of your present situation (as would be the case with us), but also the sober fact, that, at this moment it has already become evident that, for instance within and outside the circle of even our deputies (as it appears from some of their publications) there are persons, this being evident from the *propaganda* that has been released among us, who wouldn't even get the opportunity, should they emigrate, to be admitted to one of your churches in classis East. For they would not be able to give the promise as mentioned in the decision of classis East.

You must understand that during this time of discussion this change of direction doesn't only sadden us (having read your above mentioned earlier writing), but also makes the question of which direction our report to Synod must take in regard to the description of the present situation and to the direction of our advice much more difficult than any of us had anticipated when the Synod of Amersfoort gave us the mandate.

That is why we make the friendly request that your visit may be made as soon as possible. From our side we will do all we can to intensify the communications between you and us.

You will understand, brothers, that this letter is an attempt to help create clarity, which is necessary before all things. For that reason please don't separate any detail of it from its entirety, and accept our intention to help take away misunderstanding should any be present.

As we wish you the blessing of God in the preparation of internal and external decisions, we remain with brotherly greetings,

Respectfully and faithfully yours,
F. A. DEN BOEFT, chairman.
W. G. VISSER, clerk.

P.S. For convenience sake we mention the names and addresses of all the deputies, so that you can forward to all of them, if possible, the items mentioned in your letter.

Here are the names and addresses:

Rev. F. A. den Boeft, De Sav. Lohmanlaan 14a, Groningen.
Drs. R. H. Bremmer, van Nagelstraat 6, Zwolle.
Mr. P. Groen, Graaf Florisstraat 118, Rotterdam (W).
Rev. J. Hettinga, Paul Krugerstraat 9, Harlingen.
Prof. Dr. K. Schilder, Vloeddijk 14, Kampen.
Rev. W. G. Visser, Cornelis Jolstraat 56, Scheveningen.

So far the correspondence.

We don't know, whether the visit will go through. So, we will wait and see.

Scripture Index

Genesis 3 33
Genesis 17 .... 18, 30

Deuteronomy 29:29 29

1 Samuel 2:30 80

Psalm 25 54
Psalm 80 44
Psalm 112:4 80

Proverbs 8:17 80
Proverbs 16:4 124

Isaiah 5 ..... 40, 44, 50, 94-96, 143
Isaiah 5:4 94-96
Isaiah 65:16 151

Jeremiah 8:22 98

Zachariah 3:6, 7 146

Matthew 12:43 120
Matthew 22:2 119

Luke 14:6 119

John 15 .... 40, 44, 50, 94, 95
John 15:2 .... 94, 95
John 17:2 32

Acts 8 141
Acts 13:48 65

Romans 5 .... 35-37, 46
Romans 6:3, 4 49
Romans 9 .... 18, 65, 124
Romans 9:11, 12, 13 65
Romans 9:21 124
Romans 10:11 80
Romans 11 ... 40, 44, 50, 121, 124
Romans 11:17 .... 94, 95
Romans 11:17-21 44
Romans 11:33, 35 121

1 Corinthians 15 35

1 Timothy 4:1 120

2 Timothy 2:15 .... 74, 75

Hebrews 6 50
Hebrews 6:4, 5 50
Hebrews 10 50
Hebrews 10:29 50
Hebrews 12:25 150

General Index

1892 .... 16, 24, 25, 27, 28
1905 .... 23, 27
1924 ..... 25, 44, 59, 92, 101, 104,
130, 135
1944 .... 15, 26, 27, 42, 58, 82,
92, 115, 130, 154, 162
a Marck 19, 49
Aalders, G. Ch. 45, 46
Acronius 40
Alliance of Reformed
Churches 53
Amsterdam 22, 85
Apeldoorn 53
Arminian 29, 48, 52, 74, 80,
81, 84, 131, 133, 134, 139,
146, 154, 162
Arminianism 44, 47-49, 51,
52, 76, 82, 95, 125
Arminians 48, 49, 76, 80, 82,
85, 86, 90, 125
Augustijn, C. 28
Baptism(al) Form .. 59, 66, 69, 70
Barth, Karl 100
Bavinck, Herman 19, 22, 25,
28, 33, 39, 42, 51, 83, 158

Belgic Confession
Art. 14 60
Art. 22 67
Art. 24 81
Art. 24 70
Art. 31 71
Art. 33 63
Art. 33 - 35 .... 62, 67
Art. 34 63
Art. 35 64

berith 76
Berkhof, L. 19, 32, 42, 43
Berkouwer, G. C. 154
Berlin 22
Beuker, Hendericus 17, 24, 25,
28, 30, 31, 33, 35, 38, 46, 47, 53
Beza, Theodore 41, 74,
112-124, 158
Biesterveld, P. 39
Birdaard 19
Blankespoor, John 101, 103
Boer, Geert Egberts 17, 18, 20, 28
Bonhoeffer, Dietrich 45
born under the covenant 104, 105
Bos, F. L. 52
Bos, T. 27, 28
Bouwman, H. 24, 52
Bratt, J. D. 28
Bremmer, R. H. . 22, 25, 154, 167
Bruins, E. J. 20
Brummelkamp, A. . 20, 26, 27, 53
California 47, 101
Calvin, John 88, 110, 129, 130
Calvin Theological Seminary . 17,
18, 23, 25, 42, 49
Canadian Reformed
Churches 15, 17, 23, 53
Canons of Dort
I, 10 .... 64, 131, 133
I, 12 .... 133, 134
I, 17 79
I, 6, 7 61
I, 6-8 .... 60, 69
I, 7 37
I, 9 .... 128, 131, 133, 134

I, R. of E., 2 65
I, R. of E., 3 65
I, R. of E., 4, 5 134
I, R. of E., 5 65
I, R. of E., 7 134
II, 5 .... 60, 80, 112, 133,
134, 136, 137
II, 8 .... 61, 62, 67
II, R. of E., 6 60
III/IV, 1-4 60
III/IV, 8 140
III/IV, 10, 14 67
III/IV, 12, 16, 17 70
III/IV, 14 68
III/IV, R. of E., 9 70
V, 14 .... 70, 87, 150

Castellio 112, 115, 116
causal order 118
Charles V, Emperor 137-139
Christian Reformed Church 17,
20, 32, 42, 43, 52, 59,
87, 97, 101, 102, 135
church hierarchy 103
Churchill, Winston 154
classis East, (of the Protestant
Reformed Churches) 156,
157, 165, 166
Coccejus, Johannes 108
command with promise 133
common grace 40, 41, 43, 49,
59, 87, 91, 93, 96, 100-106,
109, 111, 113, 116, 122, 124,
138, 153, 158
communal grace 97, 107
condemnation 64, 66, 108,
112, 117
conditional offer 59, 104, 135
Corvinus 85, 86
Covenant (threat of the) 87, 88,
90, 110, 118, 119, 148-152
covenant-wrath 145

Covenant-breaking 145
Covenant-grace . 38, 48-51, 94-98
Dalfsen 19
Dam, R. J. 15, 27
De Cock, Helenius 18, 27, 28,
38, 53, 92
De Haan, T. F. 19, 28
De Jong, John D. 159, 160
De Klerk, Peter 17, 20, 22-24,
43, 52
de Reformatie 25, 27, 33, 45,
47, 57, 58, 94, 99, 115, 128
de Ridder, R. R. 20, 43, 52
de Wachter 18, 22, 24
Deddens, Pieter 161
Den Boeft, F. A. 167
Docter, J. 71
Doleantie 16, 25
Edinburgh 19
election 29, 32, 34, 35, 37, 38,
45, 46, 60, 64-66, 78, 82, 83,
85-87, 90, 112, 118, 128, 129,
131-133
fall of Adam 108
Fathers of Dort 76
favourable attitude 119
Ferwerd 19
Five Theses of 1905 27
Form for the Lord's Supper 70
Form for (the Administration of)
Baptism 39, 58, 59, 61,
140, 141, 143, 145, 146, 152
Form for the Installation of
Elders and Deacons 71
Francken, A. 19
Free Masonry 20
Free Reformed 18, 53
Gaffin Jr, R. B. 22, 23
Gelderland group 26, 27
Gereformeerde Kerken in
Nederland (liberated) . 45, 154
Gispen, W. H. 27

God's reliability 147, 150
God's Self-glorification 112
God's truthfulness .. 147, 150-152
Grand Rapids 17-25, 30-32,
    42, 43, 49, 53, 58, 94, 95, 156
Greijdanus, Seakle 46, 53,
    160, 161
Groen, P. 167
Grosheide-committee 98
Hallum 19
Hamilton 15, 17, 18, 20, 23,
    25, 53, 54
Hastings, J. 23
Heidelberg Catechism
    Lord's Day 3, Qu. 8 60
    Lord's Day 7 99
    Lord's Day 7, Qu. 20 66
    Lord's Day 21, Qu. 54 61
    Lord's Day 24, Qu. 64 70
    Lord's Day 25, Qu. 65 61
    Lord's Day 25, Qu. 66 . 61, 62
    Lord's Day 26 18
    Lord's Day 27 32
    Lord's Day 27, Qu. 74 62
    Lord's Day 31, Qu. 84 70
    Lord's Day 33, Qu. 91 60
    Lord's Day 45, Qu. 116 70

Hemkes, Gerrit Klaas 17, 18,
    20-22, 28, 33, 47
Hendriksen, W. 19, 42
Heppe, Heinrich 117
Hettinga, J. 167
Heyns, William Wijnand 17,
    23, 24, 28, 30-41, 43-53, 93-
    100, 106, 138, 143, 144,
    154, 158
Heynsian(ism) 47, 93, 98, 100,
    101, 104, 116, 134, 138, 158
Hoekema, Anthony A. 32, 42,
    43, 52

Hoeksema, Gertrude 156
Hoeksema, Herman 42-52, 58,
    71, 72, 74, 81, 87, 91-93, 97,
    100, 101, 103, 105-107, 109,
    110, 121, 122, 125-127, 130,
    135, 138, 153, 154, 156,
    158, 160
Hoeksema, Homer C. 43, 49
Holland, Michigan 20, 21
Holwerda, Benne 27, 156,
    159-161
Hovius, J. 53
Huisken, Wm. 71
Hulst, Lammert Jan 17-22, 27-
    31, 33, 35, 38, 40, 45-47, 49
Illinois 101
Independent Christian
    Reformed Churches 53
infralapsarian(s) 19, 26-28, 30,
    37, 43, 45, 83, 107, 108, 111,
    113, 114, 121
insusceptibility 97
internal susceptibility 95
Iowa 101
Jager, Hendrik Jan 161
Janssen, Ralph 28
Joffers, H. 26
Kalamazoo 59, 87, 104, 107,
    109, 111, 119, 121, 122, 130,
    135, 138, 160
Kampen 15, 17-28, 33, 45, 46,
    50, 52-54, 126, 137-139,
    164, 165, 167
Klooster, Fred H. 52
Kok, Bernard 159, 160
Kok, W. A. 19
Kraan, K. J. 138
Kramer, G. 41
Kreulen, J. R. 19, 27, 28, 38
Kromminga, John Henry 20
Kuiper, H. 49

Kuyper, Abraham 21, 22, 24, 25, 27, 28, 31, 39-43, 47, 50, 52, 83, 93, 113, 158

Kuyperian 21, 28, 39, 92, 96, 147, 158

liberated theology 134

Liberated Churches 92, 103, 104, 154, 160

Liberated views of the covenant and baptism 103

Liberation of 1944 ...... 15, 26, 27, 38, 47, 51, 54, 154

Lindeboom, Lukas 18, 27, 38, 53, 77

Luther, Martin 100

mission committee (of the Protestant Reformed Churches) 58, 71, 101, 102

Netherlands Confession, see Belgic Confession

New Testament .. 76, 77, 125, 150

objective 39, 40, 44, 61, 69, 95, 136, 137, 145

objective-subjective 95

Old Testament 77, 150

Ophoff, G. M. 71, 156, 160

Oud Leussen 19

Overduin, J. 18

Petter, Andrew 154, 160

Pfaltz 53

Pieters, K. J. 27, 30, 38

Plantinga, Theodore 52

Plotinus 130

Poincare 154

Polman, A. D. R. 92, 115, 162

Presbyterian Church in the United States 22

Princeton 22

Protestant Reformed Churches 47, 51, 57-59, 70-72, 82, 101-103, 114, 116, 135, 153, 156, 163

Protestant Reformed doctrine 57, 165

Protestant Reformed principles 102

Protestant Reformed Synod of 1950 58

Protestant Reformed Synod of 1951 58

Protestant Reformed theology 57, 134, 165, 166

Reformed Church in America . 20

Reformed Churches in the Netherlands (lib.) 57, 154, 163

Reformed Theological Seminary 23

regeneration 24, 28, 38, 39, 41, 43, 49, 50, 81, 84, 94, 103, 105

reliability of God ... 147, 148, 150

reprobate 43, 44, 59, 64, 104, 106-108, 116, 117, 120, 122, 151

responsibility 42, 48, 108

Ridderbos, J. 125, 138, 141, 146, 154, 162

Ridderbos, N. H. 160

sacraments 61, 62, 64, 87, 150

savour (or U.S. spelling: savor) of death 64, 100

savour (or U.S. spelling: savor) of life 64, 100

schematism 95

Schilder, A. (Mr. and Mrs.) ... 103

Schilder, H. J. 98

Schilder, Klaas 16, 25, 26, 42, 45-48, 51-53, 57, 58, 104, 154, 158, 161, 167

scolasticism 30, 95

Secession (of 1834) 15-18, 20-22, 24-29, 35, 37-39, 42, 45-49, 51-54

seed of the covenant 48, 97

Self-admiration (of God) 112
Sorbonne 129
Standard Bearer 43, 91, 92,
    101, 114, 118, 125, 134, 153,
                    156, 164, 165
Staten Bijbel (Translation) 76,
                    125, 126, 130
Strasbourg 22
subjective Covenant-
    grace 38, 48-51, 94-98
subjective grace 40, 41, 44, 94,
                    96, 97
supralapsarian(s) 19, 21, 26-28,
    43, 45, 83, 84, 87, 107, 108,
                111-121, 124, 158
supralapsarianism . 19, 21, 28, 51,
    83, 107, 110, 113, 117, 129
syllogism 147, 148
Synod of Dort 1618-19 .... 76, 130
Synod (of the Christian
    Reformed Church) of
    Kalamazoo, 1924 .... 59, 104
ten Hoor, Foppe Martin 17, 24,
    25, 28, 30-36, 38, 43, 45,
                    46, 53
Theological College of the
    Canadian Reformed
    Churches 15, 17, 18, 23, 25
Theological School in Grand
    Rapids 18, 21
Theorems 88, 116
Three Forms of Unity 27, 53,
    58, 59, 87, 92, 154, 166
Three Points of Kalamazoo 59,
    101, 102, 105, 135
total depravity 95, 97
total incapability 97
True Holland Reformed
    Church 20
truthfulness (of God)147, 150-152
Twissus 83-90, 112
Van Dam, Cornelis 15

Van der Meiden, L. H. 53
Van der Schuit, J. J. 53, 82
Van Dijk, Douwe 161
Van Hoogen, H. 28
Van Lonkhuyzen, J. 21, 42, 50
Van Mastricht 49
Van Raalte, Albertus 20
Van Til, Cornelis 22
Van Velzen, S. 20
Veenhof, Cornelis 26-28, 32,
                38, 53, 154, 161
Veltman, R. 71
veracity of God 148, 150
Visser, W. G. 158, 167
Voetius, Gisbert 19
Vollenhoven, D. H. T. 49
Vos, Geerhardus 17, 22-24, 28,
    31-35, 42, 43, 45-47, 53
Vos, Gerrit 71
Vos, Johannes G. 32
Vrijmaking (Liberation
    of 1944) 15
Wielenga, Douwe Klaas 20
Wisconsin 101
Woelderink, J. G. 34
Wormser, J. A. 27
Yoo, H. M. 19, 27
Zwaanstra, H. 17
Zwolle 20, 163, 167

Other Books from Inheritance Publications

Annotations to the Heidelberg Catechism by J. Van Bruggen
John A. Hawthorne in *Reformed Theological Journal*: . . . The individual Christian would find it a constructive way to employ part of the Sabbath day by working through the lesson that is set for each Lord's Day. No one can study this volume without increasing his knowledge of truth and being made to worship and adore the God of all grace. This book will help every minister in the instruction of his people, both young and not so young, every parent in the task of catechizing and is commended to every Christian for personal study.

ISBN 0-921100-33-7 Can.$15.95 U.S.$13.90

The Belgic Confession and its Biblical Basis by **Lepusculus Vallensis**
The Belgic Confession is a Reformed Confession, dating from the 16th Century, written by Guido de Brès, a preacher in the Reformed Churches of the Netherlands. The great synod of Dort in 1618-19 adopted this Confession as one of the doctrinal standards of the Reformed Churches, to which all office-bearers of the Churches were (and still are) to subscribe. This book provides and explains the Scriptural proof texts for the Belgic Confession by using the marginal notes of the Dutch Staten Bijbel. The Staten Bijbel is a Dutch translation of the Bible, by order of the States General of the United Netherlands, in accordance with a decree of the Synod of Dort. It was first published in 1637 and included 'new explanations of difficult passages and annotations to comparative texts.'

ISBN 0-921100-41-8 Can.$17.95 U.S.$15.90

Essays in Reformed Doctrine by J. Faber
A collection of seventeen articles, speeches, and lectures which are of fundamental importance to all Christians.
Cecil Tuininga in *Christian Renewal*: This book is easy reading as far as the English goes. It can, I judge, be read by all with great profit. . . I found the first chapter on "The Significance of Dogmatology for the Training of the Ministry" excellent. The six essays on the Church I found very informative and worth-while. . . What makes this book so valuable is that Dr. Faber deals with all the aspects of the Reformed faith from a strictly biblical and confessional viewpoint.

ISBN 0-921100-28-0 Can.$19.95 U.S.$17.90

Covenant and Election by J. Van Genderen
Even though we are familiar with the biblical promises which are also prophecies and recognize them as flowing out of the covenant the Lord made with us, we should not simply view the promise as a prediction of what the Lord is sure to do regardless of how we react to it, but rather as a promise which requires faith on our part. Basically the content of the covenant is this: I am your God and you are My people.

ISBN 0-921100-60-4 Can.$11.95 U.S.$10.90

The Covenantal Gospel by C. Van der Waal

G. Van Rongen in *Una Sancta*: . . . We would like to conclude this review with a quotation from the last lines of this - recommended! - book. They are the following: The Gospel is covenantal in every respect. If things go wrong in the churches, ask whether the covenant is indeed preached and understood. If missionary work is superficial, ask whether the covenant is taken into account. . . If sects and movements multiply, undoubtedly they speak of the covenant in a strange way, or ignore it deliberately. . . It must be proclaimed. Evangelical = Covenantal.

ISBN 0-921100-19-1 Can.\$17.95 U.S.\$16.20

The Relation Between Christian Liberty and Neighbor Love in the Church **by N. D. Kloosterman**

The winding path of this book will lead deep into the evidence of scripture, through the history of Christian ethics, and bring the reader eventually into an open clearing, looking out over the field of Christian ethics itself. Along the way one of the most surprising discoveries will be that what is 'going on' in the offense of the weak involves the relationship between Christian liberty and neighbor love. In fact, these will provide the reader with the points of reference . . .

ISBN 0-921100-30-2 Can.\$11.95 U.S.\$10.90

Church History **by P.K. Keizer**

According to Revelation 12, the history of mankind revolves around the history of Christ's Church.

Hywel Roberts in the *Banner of Truth*: . . . The author recognizes the true unity of history and relates 'the acts of God's faithfulness and lovingkindness in founding and maintaining the covenant of grace and reconciliation, a covenant that remains valid despite man's disdainful disregard.'

ISBN 0-921100-02-7 Can.\$12.95 U.S.\$11.90

Secession, Doleantie, and Union: 1834 – 1892 **by Hendrik Bouma**

In our own day, efforts toward reunion among Reformed and Presbyterian churches will succeed to the degree that the truths of Scripture, faithfully echoed by the Confessions, are truly experienced among God's people by shaping their daily obedience and motivating their piety.

But these efforts will succeed, as they did in 1892, also to the degree that we avoid elevating theological (and historical) differences to the level of the Confessions. Reformed and Presbyterian church history is replete with examples of this tragic mistake. It happens in two ways, at least: some who are "in" get pushed "out" by extra-confessional pronouncements, and some who are "out" are *kept* out by those who insist on elevating these differences to confessional status. So our modern ecumenical conversation needs the help of participants who can distinguish — without separating — theology from confession, and historical form from biblical essence. The path toward Reformed and Presbyterian (re)union will require, I think, that we live with these two equally valid, though apparently competing, claims: first, Reformed and Presbyterian believers need fewer, not more, denominations to express visibly what the Bible teaches; and secondly, genuine ecumenicity thrives on more, not less, doctrinal precision. If truth unites, then a more sure grasp of the truth should unite us more surely!

— From the *Introduction* by Nelson D. Kloosterman

ISBN 0-921100-36-1 Can.\$15.95 U.S.\$13.90

Where Everything Points to Him by K. Deddens
The Church of Jesus Christ does not live her life in isolation. Even in her corporate worship, she can be adversely influenced by the surrounding culture. Some ministers come to model themselves — even if only unconsciously — after entertainers. And some of the worshipers seem to think that a worship service is essentially a meeting between *people* in which social and aesthetic norms must prevail. In such a climate it is helpful to be reminded of the principles which have shaped corporate worship . . .

ISBN 0-921100-39-6 Can.$12.95 U.S.$11.90

Seeking Our Brothers in the Light: A Plea for Reformed Ecumenicity
Ed. Theodore Plantinga
Al Bezuyen in *Revival*: The book should well serve office bearers and lay people interested in closer contact with the liberated Churches. The work is not exhaustive but rather functions as a spring board from which further study can find a solid beginning and seeks to clear the water that must be entered if ecumenical relations are to take place between the CRC and American / Canadian Reformed Churches.

ISBN 0-921100-48-5 Can.$5.00 U.S.$4.50

Schilder's Struggle for the Unity of the Church by **Rudolf Van Reest**
Klaas Schilder (1890-1952) is remembered both for his courageous stand in opposition to Nazism, which led to his imprisonment three months after the Nazis overran the Netherlands in 1940, and for his role in the Church struggle in the Netherlands, which culminated in 1944 with the suspension of scores of office-bearers and the formation of the liberated Reformed Churches.
Thomas Vanden Heuvel in *The Outlook* of December 1990: I strongly recommend this book for everyone interested in the preservation of and propagation of the Reformed faith.

ISBN 0-921100-23-X Can.$29.95 U.S.$26.60

About Inheritance Publications

Inheritance Publications is a small company which has been established to provide Biblical Reformed literature. We want to maintain the antithesis between right and wrong, between true and false christianity. It is also our desire to give God the honour and glory due to His Name because of His covenant faithfulness. Remembering the great deeds of God in the history of His Church will always cause God's children to stand in awe for His Majesty. It is our aim to reach children with storybooks about the history of the Church, and adults with books on the doctrine of the Church. May God's Name be glorified and the readers edified by the reading of our books.